WRITING FICTION

AUGUST DERLETH

Writing Fiction

GREENWOOD PRESS, PUBLISHERS
WESTPORT, CONNECTICUT

INTRODUCTION

From the point of view of the writer, be he amateur or professional, all fiction falls into two general groups. These may be specified as realistic fiction on the one hand, and fiction which grows out of reality, on the other. These are broad classifications, and need little explanation, for it is obvious that realistic fiction is that which not only could be true in every aspect, but in many cases is, the writer having drawn upon his experience or that of others in creating it; fiction which grows out of reality may range from the simple romantic all the way to the fantastic, so long as recognizable symbols are used by the writer. Reduced to its basic essential, fiction is life, interpreted realistically or imaginatively.

The writer's approach to his subject, his treatment of his characters, his skill in infusing life into his story—all these factors and more rely on something more than the rules commonly found in copybooks and texts. This is so manifest that it seems at first consideration to be superfluous even to mention it; but it is equally manifest that the human mind at its best is fallible enough to warrant far more repetition than many of us are willing to recognize. Nor is it quite as simple as it sounds, because, while many copybooks and texts faithfully carry the rules, there is seldom mention of that something more which all too often determines the difference between a story which comes to life and one which does not.

▼

It has been said that there are but a certain number of basic plots, a certain number of basic characters, and so forth; whether or not this is acceptable to the writer, it remains no less true that the writer himself imposes his own personal limitations upon his fiction. He gains or he loses by the boundaries of his will to do, his drive, his energy, his vision, his sympathy and understanding, and, in many cases, by his perspective insofar as his abilities are concerned.

Many writers have chosen, not unwisely, to get into print through the little magazines. The editors of these magazines (apart from the cultists who go in rather heavily for prose and poetic experiments, largely meaningless and often completely lacking in social resonance) ask only sincerity and integrity with an ability to write unadorned prose; they appreciate writing skill, and they are sympathetic to any good, meaningful story, regardless of length. The fact that they do not pay for material published often blinds the beginner in writing to the less-known fact that publication in the little magazines very often pays dividends of the best to a newcomer to the ranks, for the editors of many professional magazines and of many publishing houses read these little magazines faithfully in a never-ending quest for new writers.

It is a common fallacy, chiefly fostered by the envious and unsuccessful among the writing fraternity, that it is extremely difficult, if not impossible, to reach the editorial sanctum of the average large-circulation magazine or first-rank publisher. This is simply not true. It has never been true in my experience. Within the first year of my initial publication in such little reviews as *The Midland, This Quarter, Pagany,* and *Prairie Schooner,* I had letters of inquiry about book-length work from the editors of such well-known houses as

Simon & Schuster, Houghton Mifflin, Charles Scribner's
Sons, and Harper's. Within the same period I had inquiries
about short stories from magazines of national circulation
which included *Collier's* and *McCall's*. There was absolutely
nothing in those pieces of mine which had appeared to indicate anything but an observing eye and a modest ability to
write, which, if carefully nurtured, might eventually produce
something.

The fact is that every editor in the country is constantly
vigilant and on the alert for new talent. Moreover, I have
found most editors not only patient, but extremely helpful.
Such men as Edward Weeks (Atlantic-Little Brown), Max-
well E. Perkins and William C. Weber (both of Charles
Scribner's Sons), Edward C. Aswell (Harper's), Paul Brooks
(Houghton Mifflin), and William M. Sloane III (Henry
Holt), among others, represent the finest editorial traditions,
and at the same time have every reason to be proud of their
editorial acumen, as lists of the books they have seen to press,
and of the authors whose work they have encouraged, will
show. They are not exceptions; in their constant interest in
new writers, these editors are typical of the entire profession.

The beginner in writing must learn that he cannot take
refuge in any fancy of this kind from what can be only his
own shortcomings. Publishing is a business, and the life of
any business depends upon new blood, quite frankly. Even
the best writers must die, and the publisher who has not
taken great pains to bring new names to his list will find his
business dying with his best writers. Being a businessman,
the publisher, through his editors, is not going to take any
such chance. Viewed from this realistic perspective, it must
soon be apparent to even the most gullible of writers that

there is no room for prejudice against new writers among publishers.

All this is true to an even greater degree among the magazines, and particularly among those of large circulation, where competition is so much more immediate. However, the editor of a magazine must consider to a greater extent the value of a "name" author in competing with his rivals, and there may be rare occasions when two stories of equal merit, one by an unknown writer, one by a "name" author, reach his desk. Certainly he is not to be blamed if he chooses to buy the "name" author's story instead of the newcomer's. But most astute editors are not at all likely to do anything of the sort; with one eye to the future, most editors, confronted with such a choice, would wisely buy both stories.

The beginner in writing must learn other things, quite apart from his craft.

He must strive for a sufficient perspective to enable him to look at his work with as impersonal an eye as he can muster, so that he can become his own best critic. This is by no means easy, and the writer who writes both a great deal and a great variety of work is perhaps best qualified to reach that critical objectivity which is so highly desirable in the professional writer. There is perhaps nothing more dreaded by the novice than the rejection slip; every one of us is to some degree allergic to it. I discovered this allergy as early as my third story; I found that the rejection slip had a very bad effect on my morale. One builds high hopes into every story being created, and its rejection is a blow, particularly to the beginner. I discovered that if a new story could be written before the old was rejected, my hopes for the new story acted as a kind of shock absorber in the face of the rejection of the old. This sort of armor against the rejection slip goes a long way to the development of critical perspective; it is considerably easier to examine critically a brain-child which has already taken second-place in one's affections, than it is to tear apart a one and only attempt. The writer, regardless of his field, must be a realist in regard to his work.

He must also learn to benefit by criticism. He will quickly understand that his well-meaning friends are not likely to be his best critics. He should, by the same cerebration, gather that an editor who takes time to write him a few words of criticism must have some belief in him as a writer to justify his having taken that time; and that very fact merits consideration for such criticism as has been made. He should learn that praise, no matter how sincerely given, is a heady wine and much better disregarded, and that criticism honestly made affords him a perspective on his work which he may not be fortunate enough to have, since the writer is in large part put into his work and therefore finds it difficult to dissociate himself from it. He will understand readily enough to differentiate between sincere and honest criticism on the one hand, and snide and picayune carping on the other. There are some frustrated writers hacking away at book reviewing, and they are likely to be motivated in their lesser moments by petty prejudices, but it would be unfair to judge the entire book-reviewing fraternity by isolated cases such as these.

Above all, the would-be writer must learn that nothing is so helpful a contribution toward his success as constant work. John Galsworthy, Arnold Bennett, G. K. Chesterton and scores of famous writers of our own time are on record as having felt it necessary to write—however little—

every day. A daily stint may sometimes seem very difficult and trying, but it will help to cultivate the sheer mechanics of writing, if nothing more. But it will do far more than that in pointing the way to a wider range in vocabulary, a greater compactness in writing (prolixity is generally to be avoided); it will help to develop both a sense of selection and an eye for detail, which are important; and finally, it will establish a routine, or habit if you prefer, which is not easily broken and which will come in good stead if ever the novice develops into the professional and has deadlines to meet. The development of work patterns is vital, and too much emphasis cannot be placed upon it; once a writer learns that he can write a little every day, he will do so; and once the pattern has been established, the difficulty will have gone out of it. The formation of this habit early in life made it possible for me to write my novel *Evening in Spring* in twenty days, at the rate of five thousand words a day—at the same time that I was lecturing for an hour daily at the University of Wisconsin (twenty-five miles away) on "American Regional Literature," and keeping up with all my correspondence, and my *Sac Prairie Journal* (seven hundred fifty to one thousand words daily), to say nothing of a book of poems written and revised while traveling to and from the lecture room.

This book is intended, primarily, as a modest guide to certain types of fiction, not as a compilation of directives written *ex cathedra*, but rather as an inquiry into some lesser-realized aspects of creative writing made out of one writer's experience.

CONTENTS

WRITING FICTION

I: THE REALISTIC STORY

Far too many people, writers as well as readers, think of realism as synonymous with grim tragedy. This misunderstanding arises very naturally from the emphasis placed upon the more sordid aspects of life in some of the famous novels of the genre, beginning with the work of the French Naturalists (cf.: Gustave Flaubert's *Madame Bovary*, Emile Zola's *Nana*, *The Dram-Shop*), and carried on in the fiction of the British pastoral writers (particularly in Thomas Hardy), that of the American realists of the first twenty-five years of this century (cf.: Theodore Dreiser's *Sister Carrie*, *Jennie Gerhardt*, etc., Sinclair Lewis's *Main Street*, *Babbitt*, Sherwood Anderson's *Winesburg*, *Ohio*, *Poor White*, and others), and finally in the regional writing current in America in the thirties and forties.

There is, of course, no legitimate reason for this popular misconception. The only requirement of a realistic story is that it be true to life, and, in essence, uncolored by unwarranted imagination and wishful romanticism—i. e., the "happy ending" tendency. The emphasis on stark tragedy in the late twenties and early thirties was so pronounced that Corey Ford, reviewing an O'Brien collection, parodied the realistic tale in an hilarious episode culminating in the narrator's breaking her arm "just to hear it snap." The grimness of many realistic tales of the past two decades has, in fact, done a great deal to foster the popular misconception

3

of what is realism. The railers against the formula story for pulp and slick magazines lose sight of the fact that the realistic story became a formula story to such an extent that its course could be foreseen quite as readily as that of the veriest hack-written tale, whether it appeared in one of the more eclectic little reviews or in one of the standard quality magazines.

Realism in fiction was essentially a swinging of the pendulum away from Victorian romanticism, which was fundamentally less real than a Jules Verne fantasy. Like all literary movements, realism has developed steadily from a violently truthful approach to the present-day elliptic tale weighted with imponderables and slanted directly at readers who look for between-the-lines subtleties, with symbolism in act and word playing a far greater part in the realistic story of today. It was motivated by a very honest desire to portray life as it actually was, and not as wishful readers and wishful writers hoped that it might be—and, in some cases, shunning experience, apparently believed that it was.

When writers quietly set about to write of life as they saw it all around them, breaking away from a pattern of life wishful thinkers, moralists, and romantics had imposed upon literature, they found that life was composed of many more aspects than those rose-colored and highly moral designs with which the fiction of the past century abounded. There were written then by an ever-increasing number of writers in America, particularly, ably abetted by such critics as H. L. Mencken (whose *Smart Set* and *The American Mercury* did very much to combat adverse criticism and ridiculed the lack of truth in what purported to be realistic fiction before that time), hundreds and thousands of stories designed to reveal the neglected facets of life in various parts of America. These writers had to learn by experience that such devotion to reality soon brought them up against many editorial taboos, and there came into being in America a crop of little magazines or reviews for the express purpose of printing rejected stories, either experimental or realistic. For the most part these magazines lived for but a short time; sometimes they managed to exist for a year or two, seldom longer. Most of them died within six months of the appearance of the first issue. They were published in cities and small towns in America; they were published in London, Paris, Rome, by expatriates and their friends; they bore names like *This Quarter, Tambour, Pagany, Contempo, Westminster Review, Trails,* etc., and some of them, fostered by universities and colleges, developed a special regional character and lived for many years, like *The Midland* and *The Frontier* and the still going *Prairie Schooner;* and, in the first three decades of this century, they published the work of such people as Sherwood Anderson, James Joyce, Carl Sandburg, Edgar Lee Masters, Floyd Dell, Josephine W. Johnson, and scores of other authors whose names, recited today, sound like a roster of the best-known writers in contemporary America.

These little magazines served—and in some respects still serve—a very worthwhile purpose in America; in their fostering of literary experiment, in their devotion to what they looked upon as "truthful" writing, they helped materially not only to introduce many new and important writers, but also to break down the solid bulwark of closed opinion on the subject of creative writing in America, to open editorial ranks, and to bring about such general approval that the quality magazines began to publish the same kind of stories they had once rejected, to such a degree that a reviewer of the annual O. Henry and O'Brien (now Foley) best short story collections reflected recently that there was no longer any essential difference between the short story of the little review and that of the quality magazine.

The writer alone must select the genre in which most of his writing will be done. It is not idle advice to say that a writer writes best out of his own experience, either personal or vicarious. It is necessary to live to know life, but "living" ought not to be confused with direct experience, for it is entirely possible for a hermit to bring to a subject of his choosing sympathy, understanding, and interpretation sufficiently comprehensive to reproduce life. Of the qualities necessary to a writer next to the ability and drive to work, none is more important than sympathy. Sympathy leads to curiosity and understanding and eventually to interpretation. A man who has no sympathy for his fellow human beings has no business being a writer, if one understands that by sympathy I do not mean sentimentality, but only consciousness of common bondage and appreciation of humanity.

If he is going to write about life in a realistic fashion, he has his choice of three primary types, which might be loosely described as the "hardboiled," or starkly realistic; the "expository," which includes virtually all regional writing; and the "elliptic," in which far more meaning is conveyed by implication than by what is written down.

The Hardboiled Story

The "hardboiled" school of writing is credited very largely to Ernest Hemingway. Hemingway remains its popularizer, and its chief exponent in the sense that of all those writers who have preferred to do the hardboiled story, Hemingway does it most memorably. The style is deceptively simple; it is essentially straightforward narrative, stripped of all embellishments, featuring a kind of clipped dialogue, the meaning of which is designed to grow upon the reader gradually. It is astonishingly effective, and it is not to be wondered at that scores of writers have imitated Hemingway, many of them with conspicuous success.

Examine, for instance, the beginning of Hemingway's fine story, *The Undefeated* *:

> Manuel Garcia climbed the stairs to Don Miguel Retana's office. He set down his suitcase and knocked on the door. There was no answer. Manuel, standing in the hallway, felt there was someone in the room. He felt it through the door.
> "Retana," he said, listening.
> There was no answer.
> He's there, all right, Manuel thought.
> "Retana," he said and banged the door.
> "Who's there?" said someone in the office.
> "Me, Manolo," Manuel said.
> "What do you want?" asked the voice.
> "I want to work," Manuel said.
> Something in the door clicked several times and it swung open. Manuel went in, carrying his suitcase.
> A little man sat behind a desk at the far side of the room. Over his head was a bull's head, stuffed by a Madrid taxidermist; on the walls were framed photographs and bull-fight posters.
> The little man sat looking at Manuel.
> "I thought they'd killed you," he said.
> Manuel knocked with his knuckles on the desk.

*Printed by permission of Charles Scribner's Sons.

The barren style of this opening is yet effective enough to stave off inquiry as to who or what Manuel is, what kind of building he has got into, whom he has come to see. Hemingway eschews all but the most essential description, a choice which applies even to adjectives and adverbs. He has no interest in describing Manuel before he is completely ready to do so. Not until Manuel has entered Retana's office is the reader permitted to know that *The Undefeated* will probably have to do with bull-fighting, a conclusion to which he may come because Hemingway has put in a line of deliberate description to so indicate. At the same time he may guess that Manuel is a bull-fighter looking for a bull to fight, and very probably a bull-fighter who has survived an injury.

Hemingway, in short, evinces no interest in those aspects of description which may quite as easily be supplied by the imagination of his readers. He could have made sure that nothing was left to chance. He could have begun his story in a far more usual fashion—

> Manuel Garcia was a short, lithe man with hot, brown eyes. As he climbed the steep stairs to Don Miguel Retana's office, he was weary. He set his suitcase down in the narrow hall and knocked on the bland door. There was no answer to the knock that echoed in the confined space of the hallway. Standing there in his weariness, Manuel was aware of someone near by, an indefinable conviction possessing him that, regardless of the silence, someone was in the room. He could feel it through the door, quite as if someone had moved or stirred or made some small sound.

If he had done it in this more orthodox fashion, he would certainly have lost the precision of his prose and the conciseness of his picture. Manuel Garcia comes to life quite as readily without the descriptive words and phrases which might have been added; he grows out of the imagination of his readers into a thousand different people in appearance. Yet he remains precisely what Hemingway intends him to be, and whether he has brown eyes or hazel eyes or blue eyes, and whether he is tall or short or fat or short of wind or chesty, and whether he has a lot of hair or none, and whether he is good-looking or not—all this does not alter Hemingway's Manuel Garcia in any essential detail, because Hemingway's concern is with what happens to this man, Manuel Garcia, and he allows nothing whatever to deflect him from his story—least of all such inconsequential descriptive details as contribute nothing directly to the story he has to tell.

The novice will find the hardboiled manner considerably more difficult to imitate than it would seem. For one thing, so barren a style demands the very keenest eye in the selection of detail. There are no half-way measures about it. Either the story is entirely hardboiled, or it is in a more orthodox form; it is not half of both. It takes a great deal more writing discipline to write so starkly realistic a tale as *The Undefeated* than is generally realized. Yet other writers have written successfully in the Hemingway manner, and the style has even spread from the realistic story into the genre of escape fiction, best exemplified in the detective novels of Dashiell Hammett and Raymond Chandler.

If the writer is determined to create in the style which Hemingway popularized, he must learn first of all to compress his sentences, to set down only the essential words. In this he may need practice other than the study of stories and novels in the genre, and to get that practice he might try to write poetry, which is one of the best-known exercises for the achievement of leanness in prose and the elimination of undesirable prolixity. Not a few writers have found this exercise helpful—its only potentially harmful aspect lies in the novice's tendency to regard his exercise as legitimate creation, in which case he may attempt to publish his poetry. This often-times fatal danger is scarcely likely to affect the hardier brethren, however.

Secondly, he must cultivate an eye for details. Many a story is harmed by too many details or too few. The alert novice will find out for himself which details are essential to his story, which contribute directly to his characters, his setting, and the movement of the story. A glance at the opening paragraphs of *The Undefeated* indicates that Hemingway found only a very few details necessary to his story— Manuel's suitcase, the stuffed bull's head, the framed photographs, the bull-fight posters. Apart from the names of his characters, which limited his setting to a very few countries, Hemingway's tale might have been set anywhere; only one word, put in casually, seemed to Hemingway necessary to establish that the setting of *The Undefeated* is Spain— the bull's head "stuffed by a Madrid taxidermist". Manuel's suitcase tells the reader that Manuel has come from somewhere other than the neighboring block—a nearby city, or from the country. Nothing more is necessary; the whole essential picture is there in fact and inference, and whatever other details the reader elects to fill in in his imagination cannot contribute anything at all to the story Hemingway tells.

The hardboiled story is generally a story of character, as

apart from the regional story, which is either a story of place or of character against a circumscribed background which is an integral part of the story and cannot very easily be conveyed in the stark, barren narrative style preferred by Hemingway. And, while a tough character naturally lends himself best to this particular manner of presentation, Hemingway has done equally well (contrary to his detractors) with gentle characters, so that, actually, the application of such adjectives as "tough" and "hardboiled" to Hemingway's style does an injustice to a literary artist of the first water. It was the adoption of the Hemingway manner by such people as James M. Cain (*The Postman Always Rings Twice*), Dashiell Hammett (*The Dain Curse, The Maltese Falcon,* etc.), and Raymond Chandler (*Farewell, My Lovely,* etc.) which gave meaning to the description of the manner as "hardboiled".

While generally not as subtle as the elliptic narrative currently so popular, such Hemingway followers as John O'Hara and Jerome Weidman—distinguished authors in their own right, and by no means to be thought of as imitators—have demonstrated, quite as well as Hemingway himself, that subtlety and stark, barren realism need not be antipodal.

The Hemingway manner has appealed very largely to many writers who belong to what is known as the "Proletarian" movement—i. e., that school of writers devoted to writing about the social adjustments of our time, to the exposition of such social problems as sharecropping, unfair labor practices, infringements upon civil liberties, racial and religious intolerance, etc., but few of them have come forth with stories fully in the Hemingway pattern, preferring instead to infuse their realism with long descriptive passages rather in the Continental manner, grim and humorless, and to keep to the Hemingway pattern only in dialogue, where it is admittedly most effective. They are thus not so much "hardboiled" realists as propagandists, and few of their books succeed as art, however much they may succeed as propaganda. Such exceptions as Upton Sinclair's pre-Hemingway *The Jungle*, John Steinbeck's *The Grapes of Wrath*, Robert Cantwell's *The Land of Plenty*, Albert Halper's *Union Square*, and Jack Conroy's *The Disinherited* are noteworthy performances the beginning writer might do well to read in order to familiarize himself with first-rate fictional treatments of contemporary social problems with which he himself may want to deal as he matures in his chosen field.

Regional Writing

Current emphasis on "regionalism" tends to obscure the fact that "regionalism" is little more than a label for the contemporary phase of that same loose movement in American letters which began with Dreiser's Naturalism and flowered into the realism of the Midwestern literary renaissance of this century's second decade. It is a label more or less specifically applied to those historical, bucolic, or social novels, poems, plays, etc., which bear upon them the unmistakable mark of our various American regions—the Midwest, the South, the Border States, the New England country, the Plains States, the West—subdivided into Northwest, Southwest, and the Coastal region.

The writer who approaches regionalism new to the label will find outstanding writers representative of their own regions. The formative four were, of course, Midwesterners —Theodore Dreiser, Edgar Lee Masters, Sherwood Anderson, and Sinclair Lewis; these, followed by Willa Cather, Robert Frost, Carl Sandburg, and a handful of others, wielded the most influence upon the regional writers of the twenties and thirties. Typical of Midwestern regional writers of today are Ruth Suckow, Paul Corey, Phil Stong, and Harold Sinclair; of the New England country, LeGrand Cannon, Gladys Hasty Carroll, W. W. Christman, Robert P. Tristram Coffin, Walter D. Edmonds and John Gould Cozzens; of the Border States, Ellen Glasgow, Caroline Gordon, Paul Green, Harry Harrison Kroll, Andrew Lytle, James Still, Jean Thomas, and Jesse Stuart; of the South, Hamilton Basso, Ben Lucien Burman, William Faulkner, William March, Caroline Miller, Julia Peterkin, and James Street; of the Plains States, Dora Aydelotte, George Milburn, J. Hyatt Downing, C. P. Lee, and Dorothy Thomas; of the Southwest, Mary Austin, Paul Horgan, Oliver La Farge, Flannery Lewis, Mari Sandoz, and Paul Wellman; of the Coastal-Northwest, Archie Binns, H. L. Davis, Vardis Fisher, Nard Jones, John Steinbeck, and Stewart Edward White.

The quality of universality must be an integral essential of the good regional novel or short story, just as much as of any good writing. The region, in short, must be secondary to story and character development. The paradox of regional writing is that when it is consciously done, it seldom succeeds. There is, of course, good reason for this, for, when the writer's attention dwells primarily on the region, he may lose sight of his story and of his characters.

"Regionalism" has never been a conscious movement, even though it is usually spoken of in terms of such a movement. Little reviews were publishing regional fiction long before the term was used, and such pioneer professors in exploring regional writing as Howard Odum, John T. Frederick, and B. A. Botkin, began to use the label consciously only as the thirties approached, and it was apparent that many works of prose and poetry indelibly and faithfully mirrored their regions of origin. For each region has certain essential differences, not only of climate and topography, but of economic and social problems, and of peoples.

It is true that, fundamentally, people are very much the same, but there are environmental differences which emerge tellingly in various regions, and there are economic problems, like those of sharecropping, industrialization, the Dust Bowl tragedy, etc., which are specifically regional, and people are profoundly affected by them. The writer of regional prose must know what has gone into the history of his region, what has influenced his people, what is responsible for their thought-patterns; he must know, in short, what specific problems determine what they say and do, and fix the patterns of their lives.

Unfortunately, the beginner in regional writing, who has heeded the adage that he must write about what he knows best, is all too often deceived by the merely superficial aspects of his region. A good regional novel is not written solely out of dialect differences, for instance; nor is it written out of quaint customs. No writer has been more successful than Jesse Stuart (winner of the Thomas Jefferson Southern Award for 1944 for his *Taps for Private Tussie*, Book-of-the-Month Club Selection for December 1944) in skillfully utilizing his native Kentucky speech patterns in his prose and verse, though James Still, also of Kentucky, comes close to Stuart's excellence. But these writers are the manifest exceptions, because they have never lost sight of the fact that, however prominent speech patterns may be in their books, character and story must come first.

Stuart and Still, incidentally, have been widely published in such magazines as *Esquire, The Saturday Evening Post, Collier's, The Household, The Yale Review, Harper's, Story, Scribner's*—magazines representing the slick-paper, the quality, and the little review markets; and both have been represented in the *O. Henry Prize Stories* and the O'Brien (now Foley) *Best Short Stories* annuals. The range of the Stuart-Still publications indicates that the good regional story is as much desired by the so-called slick-paper magazines as by the quality magazines. Examination of a few typical Stuart stories will show that Stuart's situations and people have a universality of appeal completely apart from their setting, which is always unmistakably the Kentucky or Border State milieu.

Regional writing may be contemporary or historical. The historical regional novel is perhaps best exemplified in the work of Walter D. Edmonds, whose novels are among the finest of their kind in contemporary letters. Upstate New York, with emphasis on the Erie Canal country, has been the exclusive province Edmonds has chosen to exploit, and he has written about it in short stories and novels with a singular devotion and a scholar's attention to history, both in the larger sense of events, and in the smaller of customs, mores, etc. His work, too, has been widely published in both slick-paper and quality magazines.

The regional historical novel, of course, differs markedly from the costume novel, which is also historical. *Anthony Adverse* and *Gone with the Wind* are costume novels with a wide range of action, and an emphasis on picaresque adventure, action, or history as history, while Edmonds's novels are meticulous—but never apparently so—in their concern with the way people lived in the periods of their settings.

The regional historical novel, however, offers some rather individual problems for the writer. The emphasis on history ought to be subordinated to the story in proper perspective; that is to say, the regional writer ought not to write a record of historical events, but rather a record of what people thought, said, did in the time-period of his novel. For that reason, he must look upon historical events and personages more or less as the people of that day looked upon them; and that perspective he gets best not from historical records, but from the editorial and news columns of old newspapers and contemporary journals, diaries, letters. Manifestly, access to a good newspaper file is an asset, for the editorials usually reflect the concerns of the people. There are, too, certain references which are of help in the same way, that is, directing attention to popular customs of the day, and to the concerns of the man in the street as opposed to those of history as we usually understand that word—Mark Sullivan's *Our Times*, Fred Lewis Pattee's *The Feminine Fifties*, Frederick Lewis Allen's *Only Yesterday*, Thomas Beer's *The Mauve Decade*, Meade Minnigerode's *The Fabulous Forties*, for example. And, in addition to these, are the accounts of contemporary travelers; in my own *Sac Prairie Saga*, I have found most useful such narratives as the *Jesuit Relations*, Captain Marryat's *A Diary in America*, Frederika Bremer's *America of the Fifties*, etc.

It is too often true that the writer makes the initial mistake of looking upon an historically great person as contemporarily great within his own time, and such is seldom the case.

Lincoln has been especially so treated by many novelists. The same mistake is made of events, in regard to which very seldom does anyone know at the time of their occurrence how large they will loom in the light of later history. Writers who lose sight of these facts risk major criticism and loss of prestige. It should be conceded, however, that fewer writers are making these errors today than did so twenty or only ten years ago. It is not too much to say that the excellent work done by such writers as Walter D. Edmonds has set the pace in the field of the regional historical novel.

The regional writer will do well to be assured of his background before he begins to write. That is, he should know the facts of history, local and national, whether or not he intends to utilize those facts, for any given period. It has been my own experience that ten thousand words of concise notes have sometimes eventually yielded less than ten lines scattered throughout a finished novel; nevertheless, in those notes have been the facts of, say, a decade's history—the decade of the novel—and the feeling of the times culled from the sources and references mentioned above; and a thorough understanding of that history and feeling of the times must inevitably be transmitted to the reader in the completed novel, whether or not direct reference is made to specific historical events. Indeed, the regional writer succeeds best when he makes only casual, indirect references; but those references should never be dragged in by the heels. The interested writer might compare in the light of this assertion, my *Still Is the Summer Night* (1937) with *Shadow of Night* (1943).

The regional story, short or long, must never be superimposed upon a background of history, customs, mores, etc., but must seem to grow naturally out of that background for, if the background takes precedence either in unseemly emphasis upon history or customs, or in descriptive passages, the novel must inevitably fall by the wayside. Its characters must be as true to life in one area of the country as in another; they may manifest speech differences, custom differences, and the like, but fundamentally they must be always first and foremost good, convincing, universally identifiable characters. Jesse Stuart's hill people, Walter D. Edmonds's canallers, Ruth Suckow's farmers are as recognizable to common human experience in Alabama as in Oregon, in Arizona as in Maine; but no reader, taking up the books in which these characters appear, and postulating the elimination of all place names, would fail to identify their native regions within the regional boundaries of, respectively, Kentucky, New York, and Iowa.

The beginner in regional writing might do well to study some of the successful regional writing of today. He might turn to Stuart, Still, Suckow, Edmonds; he might study village mores as seen in the novel best in Zona Gale's *Birth,* and in journal form in my own *Village Year.* If he is writing about rural life, he might contrast Louis Bromfield's *The Farm* to the three novels making up Paul Corey's trilogy of the Mantz family in Iowa; he might study the sharecropper problem in such a novel as Paul Green's *This Body the Earth,* the problem of the Indian minority in Oliver La Farge's *Laughing Boy,* the problem of industrialization in Sherwood Anderson's *Poor White;* he might wish to know intimately the little tragedies and joys of little lives in such notable masterpieces as Edgar Lee Masters' *Spoon River Anthology* and Sherwood Anderson's *Winesburg, Ohio.*

Having seen what other writers have done with their own regions, the novice need only apply the measure of his own experience to his own region, and begin writing—all other factors being equal. He will learn that writing the regional story cannot be done consciously, as I have pointed out; he must first be so thoroughly imbued with the aspects of life which go to make up his specific region that those aspects show through any story he tells as naturally and as easily as the story itself emerges. Once he has mastered that fundamental—knowing his own region and expressing it without conscious effort—he can turn his attention to the development of his story and his characters with the end in view of writing a good story—*not* of writing a good regional story.

What this amounts to, of course, is nothing more than adding to the old adage that a writer should write of what he knows best, that he should not let himself be blinded by what he knows. In short, no writer sets out to write a regional story; he sets out, if he is wise, to write a good story, with a regional background as incidental.

From the point of view of the novice, it becomes necessary to determine just what is entailed in the adequate presentation of his region. Some indications have already been made, specifically the social problems of individual regions, and the formative influences of regional history. Dialect variations, colloquialisms, social customs and mores are the obvious aspects, of course. But without a thorough knowledge of his region's history, the beginner in fiction may well be tripped up by these seemingly obvious aspects in that he may very well mistake manifestations of folk customs for regional differences. If he is informed about the nationalities (and their folk customs) which have filtered into his home region, he will learn readily enough to differentiate between the unadulterated customs of other nationalities and those which have grown naturally with the generations.

To a certain extent, colloquialisms grow out of attempts to translate foreign idioms freely; on occasion foreign words or phrases are adopted into colloquial English; in the case of the latter, they are likely to be non-regional, existing wherever the parent language has been carried over into the New World; in the former, however, they may very well be regional in character. The writer himself must determine this, and he can do so by checking against such references as the *Oxford English Dictionary,* H. L. Mencken's *The American Language, The American Thesaurus of Slang,* etc. Common expressions of speech may vary from one region to another, and sometimes within regions. Such a usual expression as "I'll be dog-goned" readily becomes "I'll be dogged" and "I be dog' "; "I could have died laughing" becomes "I 'most died" or "I like to died"; etc. The writer will use these sparingly, and always with the utmost naturalness.

It is a common failing of the writer to be careless in his observations of life. Observation cannot be emphasized too much. If you are going to write about life, you must both live and observe it; you must not shrink from any aspect of life, and above all, you must not blind yourself to such facets as do not appeal to you. Nothing betrays carelessness in a regional writer quite so much as his use of dialect. Overuse of dialect is to be frowned upon, of course; too much dialect mitigates against reader-interest, detracts from the story, and eventually palls on the reader. Next to overuse in the roster of possible errors is inconsistency in speech patterns. This is usually most obvious in the common and not regionally restricted dropping of participial endings. The character who says "comin' " is not likely suddenly to say "coming"; on the other hand, it does not follow that he will also say "callin' " instead of "calling". Only meticulous observation will give a writer the feeling of speech in his home region.

This is no less true of social customs, traditions, mores. Infiltrations from abroad are readily enough identified, and are not essentially regional, since they may have been carried into every corner of the United States; but it should be noted that locality variations of such folk practices are regional in character. Festival practices, wakes, folk picnics—all may be importations; but the mutations are very probably authentically regional. The growth of new customs lending color to life in any region helps to define and portray the character of such a region; it is the creative artist's task to isolate such life-patterns.

But anyone who depends upon his memory alone is guilty of folly. Since the regional writer must first of all be a student of his region, it is decidedly not inapropos for him to carry a notebook or to keep a journal. I have myself kept a journal for a decade; I have found it extremely helpful. Now approaching the two-million-word mark, with part of it already in book form and other portions coming, I have duly recorded a great variety of details, all of which have proved to be very useful—colloquialisms, local superstitions, village customs, village mores, credos, thumb-nail epitaphs of local lives, data on bird migration, frog calls, bird songs, the growth of flowers, behavior patterns, local history and lore, etc. Though not intended as such, the *Sac Prairie Journal* forms an integrated picture of Midwestern village life.

Perhaps more than any other, the regional writer must

exercise realistic selection. There are some writers in the field who put down word for word and word after word what their chosen characters have said, with deadly effect. This is not creative writing, of course; this is reporting, and it should not be confused with creative fiction. The writer creates fully as much in his omissions as in what he sets down; a story may be told far more effectively, and with no less realism (or regionalism) in ten sentences out of a possible hundred the characters of real life used.

It seems hardly necessary to point out that the conventional formulae are just as much to be avoided in good regional writing as elsewhere. There was a time when the pioneer novel had a set, grim pattern—a pioneer family came into their chosen wilderness home; there was trouble with 1) the Indians; 2) rascally white men bent on exploiting either a) the Indians or b) the settlers; this was hardly overcome when drought, prairie fire, locusts, or floods ruined the crop on which they were depending for the winter; and after this everything possible could happen—Indians, if there were any, went on a rampage and scalped pa; the cow died; ma got sick and almost died—and little Jody had to carry on alone, eventually to come through with a whopping good crop, almost to a fanfare of trumpets. This pattern, with endless variations, was repeated so persistently that city book reviewers swallowed it hook, line and sinker as the genuine article, to such a degree that when a really original and more authentic regional pioneer novel came along, these good if hoodwinked reviewers looked down their noses at it and trumpeted that, of course, everyone knew that pioneering was a grim business and these pioneers had things much too easy, ergo, the book in question was not very good and the poor author had better "study his background." This was either a backhanded tribute to the formulae devotees, or an indictment, however unwitting, of the perspicacity of the reviewers. We have progressed even in the regional novel from such undue emphasis on conflict with the elements and the environment to somewhat more emphasis on conflict within one's self, with the felicitous result that the regional novel of today is likely to offer much more to the reader than the average regional novel of the early thirties.

The Elliptic Story

The elliptic story may or may not be indirect, but usually is. It is primarily a story in which the real theme is presented symbolically or behind a screen of events which are in themselves a superficial story, the implications of which are more important than the actual narrative told. It is, in short, weighted, and what is told between the lines is the real heart of the story.

The elliptic story has been in vogue for some time. Probably more such stories appear in *The New Yorker* and *Mademoiselle* than elsewhere, but *Harper's Bazaar, The Atlantic Monthly, Harper's* and most of the quality magazines and little reviews have printed them with persistence and very often with conspicuous success. It should be noted that the successful stories in the genre are most usually the product of skilled writers—not necessarily well-known writers. There is something of the same paucity of exposition, the same compactness of dialogue about most of the elliptic stories that there is in the better stories of the so-called hardboiled school.

The writer's primary guide, of course, is to determine the

most effective indirect approach to the point he wishes to make. His principal danger is of over-weighting his story, reducing it to absurdity by either making it too obvious or too subtle on the one hand, or by taking a point or a theme which is not really meritorious on the other. Manifestly, the elliptic story is very seldom a story of orthodox plot; it may be, but most often it is described by critics as "an expanded anecdote", a "sketch" or a "fragment". Reduced to its essentials it is an elliptic narrative in which selected symbols, events, or words are utilized to underline a thesis. Racial intolerance even among those who talk against it, for instance, may be the real theme of a seemingly rambling tale of a Negro's unsuccessful attempt to get himself a job in a Northern college town. Or a brittle narrative of the little words and deeds of a lady introduced to the reader as a champion of Christianity, and on the surface seeming to be so, may be designed to show that her entire life is not at all truly Christian. In the former story there may be no direct mention or hint of racial intolerance; in the latter, not one expressed doubt about the heroine's Christianity. But these things exist between the lines for any alert reader to see.

One of the best and most direct examples of the elliptic story is *Blockbuster,* by Mark Schorer, originally printed in *Mademoiselle,* reprinted in the *O. Henry Memorial Award Prize Stories of 1944.* Mr. Schorer, who has written two fine novels—one in the regional-historical field (*A House Too Old*), one in the province of social mores (*The Hermit Place*), is one of the most competent and skilled younger writers in the field of the short story. His first collection, *The State of Mind,* appears early in 1946. *Blockbuster* is vorthy of such extended examination as can be given it only through a reading.

BLOCKBUSTER*

by Mark Schorer

"Today, today," Dickie Morris said again, quietly, almost musingly, and no one in the room looked up at him. His sister Margie sat on the floor, busy with a parade of wooden animals she had removed from a crèche under the Christmas tree; his mother was reading on the sofa; and his father was still completely hidden by the Sunday newspaper. "Today's the day," the boy said, and turned to a window. He looked out at the suburban street, piled high with new snow, brilliant in winter sunshine, and he watched a man in a blue mackinaw pulling a boy on a sled, and a setter leaping beside them over drifts. He heard the newspaper rattling behind him, and he whirled round to see that his father had dropped it. "Now?" he cried.

Dan Morris yawned and stretched out his arms.

"Sleepy?" Kitty Morris asked, looking up.

"I woke up at four and couldn't get back to sleep."

"You were sleeping at seven."

"Yes. Finally."

"What was wrong?"

"I don't know. Nerves."

"You—nerves?"

"Draft nerves, I suppose."

"Now, Dad?" Dickie asked, crowding between his father's knees.

Dan hugged him briefly. "Wait just a second." He

* Reprinted by permission of Mark Schorer, from *Mademoiselle*.

hunted through the rumpled pile of newspaper, pulled out the front section and walked over to the chintz-covered sofa where Kitty sat reading. Her legs were pulled up under her, and she had not pinned up her hair which hung loosely and unevenly about her neck, and she looked young in her white housecoat.

He sat down beside her and pointed to a column of print. "I can still be called up any time. See?"

Kitty glanced at the newspaper and said quickly "It's just the same as it was, isn't it? Isn't it just the same? They won't actually be needing you yet awhile."

"Kit, we've been all through this, time and again But—well, I can't see ahead for *you*, even now. And of course I want to do my share. If they need me I'll go—of course." He was looking around the pleasant living room, flooded with morning sunshine, at the garlands of tinsel on the tree and the holly strung in the door-ways, and suddenly he reached out and seized Margie who had left her animals and was standing before him and held her against his chest.

Dickie was watching. "What's going to happen?" he asked.

"Nothing, dear," Kitty said.

"How about that train, Dick?" Dan asked abruptly The children followed him into the small sun parlor off the living room. It was empty; rug, furniture, and plants had all been removed, everything but the green and yellow flowered draperies.

"How're you going to do it?" Dickie asked as he stared at the sheets of plywood stacked against the wall

"Just nail them down. Let's see—hammer, nails screwdriver, tacks for the tracks, tack hammer—you bring the tracks from under the tree."

"They're here, they're all ready, they've been wait-ing—"

"Trains, too? Okay. I'll get the tools." He went out

"Dickie," Kitty called. She patted the place beside her on the sofa. "Sit here, dear."

"You read to me, Mummie?" Margie asked, holding a book she had picked up from under the tree.

"Six-year-olds," Kitty said emphatically to the boy, "almost always have the wind-up kind of train, and—"

"But *mine's* electric," Dickie exclaimed.

"Yes, but the point is, Dickie, that you really are too young. Only we thought we couldn't get another until after the war, and that may be quite a while. Even the plywood, you see, Dickie, was hard to get. You can't just call up and get things any more."

"Why did we need the plywood?"

"The floor is warped, and an electric train needs a smooth floor. You've been very patient—"

"What does the war need plywood for?"

"I don't know. Airplanes to bomb the Nazis. No, it couldn't be planes. Gliders, perhaps. But the point is, Dickie," she said firmly, "we expect you to take care of the train as though you were eight or ten, a big boy."

Dan came back with the tools. He had put on sneakers and an old gray flannel shirt. Dickie jumped to his feet.

The panels of plywood had been cut to the shape of the sun parlor, and in a few minutes Dan had them in place and started to nail them down. Kitty pulled a chair up to the french doors of the sun parlor and sat down with the newspaper. The children crowded round their father as he moved about on his knees.

"Don't eat those nails," Dickie said happily.

Dan glanced at him and grinned, the nails between his teeth, and went on pounding. Finally he stood up. "There, Dick, that's done. Now where are the tracks?"

Margie stood beside her mother. "You read to me?" she asked, fidgeting on one leg and still holding her book. When her mother did not look up from the newspaper Margie went back to the tree and pushed the in tricately carved sheep and cows into a heap.

"How's that?" Dan asked when the tracks had been laid out in a large oval in the center of which he squat ted with his son.

" 'Christmas week bombings terrific,' " Kitty read aloud. She looked up. "Can anything be left of those cities, anything at all?"

Dan came into the living room and took a cigarette from a box.

" 'Blockbuster'!" said Kitty, and shuddered. "What a dreadful word! Oh, Dan, what'll we do when—"

Dickie, who had been listening to them, came out with two pieces of track in his hands. "Is this the way?" He tried to join them.

"Just a second, Dick. Let me have this cigarette." To Kitty he said, "When I go—"

Margie looked up from the animals. "Where you going, Daddy?"

"This isn't the time, I guess," Dan said to Kitty.

"You want to be a soldier, Dad?" Dickie asked, look ing at him with interest.

"Who said anything about being a soldier?"

"Would we move? Could I take the train? I could be a soldier!"

"Come on, let's get the tracks together." He stamped out his cigarette and they went back into the sun parlor and Dan began to join the sections of track.

"I'll help," Dickie said. He tried to fasten two pieces of track and was still struggling with them when Dan half the oval completed, grasped one of them. "Oh," he said, and crawled around the circle to work the other way.

At last Dickie got his two pieces together and began to fasten them to the large section which Dan had al ready finished. He lifted the end of the arc of track off the floor and it suddenly fell apart. Dan looked up, and his jaws tightened. He spoke in a low, exasperated voice. "Damn it, Dick, that's not helping. I don't intend to work at this thing all day."

Dickie dropped the track and looked at the floor. "It's my train," he murmured.

Dan stood up. "Okay, you set it up." He started to walk away. Dickie watched him despairingly.

"Or do you want to let me do it?" Dan asked firmly.

"You do it," Dickie said, and slid back against the wall.

Then, as something snapped and crackled in the living room, they turned to look. Margie had stepped on the fragile animals, and two of them lay on the floor in splinters.

"Oh, Margie!" Kitty wailed, standing over them. "Those were mine! I've had those ever since I was *little!* You just won't learn to keep away from my *things*." She swooped down and picked up the child. "You sit in the hall until you really *want* to be in here with us," she said. Margie was howling.

Kitty plumped her down on the bottom step of the stairway in the hall and came angrily back into the living room. She picked up the fragments of painted wood and looked at them in her hands. "How maddening! My grandmother brought these things to me from Switzerland when I was a little girl. Really—"

Dan was grinning a little. "Things," he said. "Do things matter?" And the smile left his face as once more he looked lingeringly at the living room, and his eyes fastened on the wax flowers under a Victorian glass dome on the mantel. "I guess they do," he said.

Kitty dropped the wreckage into a wastebasket. "No," she said, "they don't, of course."

In the hall Margie was sobbing, and Dickie was looking at his mother accusingly. "She didn't *mean* to do it."

Kitty stared at him and suddenly she said, "Of course she didn't! Things! Dickie, I'm ashamed of myself. Losing my temper over a few broken sheep. Oh, I *am* ashamed! Margie, come back," she called, and sat down again. Margie, sniffling, walked stiffly past her mother and on into the sun parlor where Dan was fastening the track to the plywood with carpet tacks. Dickie had emptied all the cartons which had been stacked in a corner, and put their contents in the center of the oval —the transformer, the tunnel, the trains—engine, coal car, tanker, gondola car, and caboose. They looked bright and new in the sunlight.

"This piece isn't very definite, Dan. I still don't believe they'll need you for a while," said Kitty.

"Why don't you face it, Kit? And forget it."

The newspaper rattled into her lap and her face suddenly seemed much older. "But, Dan—I don't mean I want to keep you here—if they need you. I'm sure I could find *some* work somewhere, and the children—"

"I want you to look at this engine," Dan said abruptly to Dickie.

"I did—lots," he said absently, but he was staring at his mother, and he asked, "What did you say?"

"Look at it closely," Dan said, tugging at his sleeve. He picked up the engine. It was solid and heavy, beautifully designed, a perfect model. "Look in there, Dick. Delicate as a watch. You've got to handle it carefully."

"I know it."

"Well, let's connect the transformer." He pulled a jackknife and a coil of fine wire from his pocket, cut the wire into two even lengths, pared the insulation off the ends, connected the two bare ends with the plate fastened under the tracks and the two other ends with the transformer. "Now we line up the trains." He put all the cars on the track and joined the fine couplings. "Now you have to be sure that all the wheels are on the track, and especially these."

The children and their father were all on their knees, staring under the engine.

"Now look at this," Dan said, pointing to a small lever on the top of the engine. "When it's in the middle it's in neutral. This side is reverse. This side is forward. Always have it in the middle when you plug in the transformer. Then move it to forward. See?"

Dickie nodded breathlessly.

"Plug in the transformer," Dan said, pointing to an electric outlet in the baseboard.

Suddenly the little headlight on the engine flashed on and the motor began to hum. "There she is," Dan said. "Ready?"

The children were hopping with excitement.

"Okay!" Dan pushed the lever. The train began to move, then quickly picked up speed, and, when it reached the first curve in the oval track, rushed off, dashed against the wall, and toppled on its side, its wheels spinning and the motor buzzing loudly.

"Too much speed," Dan said. He adjusted the switch on the transformer, picked up the cars, put them back on the tracks, connected those that had become uncoupled in the spill, and said, "All right, here we go." Once more he moved the lever.

Just then Margie screamed, "The tunnel!" She grabbed the forgotten tunnel and put it over the track, but before she could straighten it the train had bumped into it and once more crashed off the tracks, all the cars on their sides again, the wheels spinning.

"God damn it," Dan said. "All right, Margie. You get off there to the side and stay put. There are too many of us here."

"Come out with me," Kitty called, but Margie backed against the windows of the sun parlor and stood there

Once more Dan put the train in order, and this time it stayed on the track until it came to the curve. Once more it dashed across the floor, against the wall, and spilled.

"Still too fast," Dan said.

He adjusted the transformer and went through the whole business again. This time the train barely crept along the track, but it went around the entire oval, and then for the second time passed safely over the treacherous curve. Dan touched the transformer, and the train picked up a little speed. Margie came closer, and both children jigged with excitement, and when the engine came to the curve it crashed once more.

"God damn it!" Dan cried, loudly this time. He bent down closely over the crucial curve and examined the tracks. "Nothing wrong here," he said. "They're tight as anything."

"Dan," Kitty said from the door.

"Let's try it again. Now both of you keep quiet. Don't hop up and down."

Dickie and Margie stood side by side against the wall and watched Dan put the cars together again and push the lever. Slowly the train started forward and picked up speed. As it came toward them both children held their breath, clenched their fists tightly, and then, as it passed them, began to jig. The train dashed off the tracks at the curve.

Dan was kneeling tensely in the center of the oval. His face was bright red. He seized the engine in his hand and began to shout at the children. "God *damn* it, can't you do as you're told? I told you not to hop! You *shake* it off! Do you want this damned train or don't you? I'll *smash*—"

"*Dan!*" Kitty cried.

He looked up at her. Then he looked at the children. Margie's lips were trembling and tears were in her eyes, but Dickie was standing up straight, his eyes meeting his father's, staring at him.

"Dan," Kitty said.

He put the train down, pulled the plug of the transformer, and walked out. Kitty followed him into the dining room.

"Dan," she said, "it wasn't the children. I tried to tell you. From where I sat I suddenly saw that the plywood right there slopes, just the way the floor under it does. We'd better get a carpenter."

Dan's face was white now, and his hands were trembling as he clutched the neck of a decanter and poured whisky into a tall glass. He drank it quickly.

"You mustn't lose your temper that way, especially over objects. It really was the engine you were outraged about, not the children. You really mustn't, Dan. Oh, darling . . ."

He looked away from her at the leaves of the laurel wreath in the center of the mahogany dining table. "Holidays! It wasn't even the engine, I'm afraid. Kit, I'm losing my—"

"What's that pounding?"

Then Margie was crying out to them from the door of the dining room. "Dickie's—Dickie's—Dickie is—" She could not finish what she was trying to say, but her parents did not wait. They rushed past her, through the living room, to the doors of the sun parlor. They saw Dickie kneeling on the floor, Dan's heavy hammer in his hands, slamming it over and over with methodical fury on what was left of the engine, and shouting, "I'm a Nazi bomber! I'm a Nazi bomber!"

Dan, leaning weakly against the doorframe, watched him without saying anything. But Kitty was crying.

Dickie looked up. His face was red, and he was biting

his lip. He lifted the hammer again and struck it with a bang against the wreckage. Defiantly he lifted it once more, but this time he brought it down less heavily. Then, still looking at his parents, he began to cry. "I'm ashamed," he sobbed as the hammer fell from his hands. The tears streamed down his flushed face, and he sobbed again, "I'm ashamed! I'm ashamed!"

Dan dropped to his knees and seized the boy's hands. "No, don't be, Dickie, don't be, please," he whispered urgently. "I'm the one, Dickie, I'm the one."

"And I," Kitty said, "and I. Dickie—we're the ones."

On the surface of this orthodox short story, the narrative concerns a mounting friction brought about by uncertainty in the draft status of Dan Morris. The reader will observe that it follows the traditional story form—conflict, however subtle, is immediately apparent; it mounts to a brief climax; there is a quick ending in which the larger theme of the story is conveyed. The theme is, clearly, one of adult responsibility in the world of childhood, and, beyond that, the implication of adult responsibility throughout the world. Note how admirably Mr. Schorer uses his four characters as foils—Dickie and Margie almost exactly pattern Dan and Kitty; Margie is a foil for Dickie and Kitty is a foil for Dan. The conflict is sharpened by the violence instilled in Dickie by Dan's own violence. Unaware of the complete meaning of his father's violence, the boy responds in a more primitive way and so points up the theme of adult responsibility in a world of peace or war. "The father, under the draft-threat strain, unfairly lashes out at the child," writes Mr. Schorer in analysis. "The child carries on where the father leaves off, but with the significant inversion, or addition, of fancying himself a 'Nazi bomber'—that is, he identifies himself with the side of cruelty, aggression, destruction, and mistaken righteousness, and at the same time, in his 'I'm ashamed,' has been forced to take on the burden of the guilt." Despite the emphasis on war and wartime status, the war is only an incident in *Blockbuster*.

Because such a story entails a great deal of subtlety, it succeeds best in the short length, or at most, in novelette length. Successful novels in the genre are very few. It is manifest that most of the stories which can be classified as "elliptic" are slanted at highly literate and intelligent readers, but the aspect of *Blockbuster* which makes it more memorable from the point of view of technique alone, is that it can be enjoyed quite as well without any comprehension of its hidden meaning. Schorer scorns the weighted word and phrase, by and large; he simply illustrates his thesis, and his story exists on two planes, either one of which is noteworthy, and each of which is complete within its own boundaries.

A manifest danger of writing elliptic stories lies in being over-subtle, in studying words and phrases until the real meaning of the story is so concealed that it is not readily apparent, much in the manner of many so-called "semanticists" or "classicists" in poetry, whose concern with words, word-meanings and form is such that their poetry reaches new heights of obscurantism. That the same result has often been achieved by experimenters in the field particularly of the elliptic story can be discovered by an examination of the files of many little magazines, particularly the "advance guard" or experimental publications. The average novice is not likely to write elliptic stories unless his natural bent is in their direction; they offer too many difficulties in addition to fundamental mastery of plot structure and narrative technique, representing as they do rather a refinement of standardized narrative technique.

In General

Regardless of what kind of realistic story he may choose to write, the beginner must settle for himself just what he will do about certain problems which will inevitably arise, far more often in the writing of realistic fiction than in any other kind of writing. He must determine, primarily, just how "real" his story is going to be. That is his chief problem, and it has various aspects.

For one thing, if his story is based on life, he must have a thorough knowledge of the legal aspects of writing about real-life people, so that he can avoid legal complications— libel, slander, etc. Even more important in this connection is the necessity of avoiding needlessly hurting people. Regardless of what he may think about his work, the artist has a moral and ethical obligation in this respect; this is far too often overlooked. I do not, of course, have reference to people who are subject to hypersensitivity, fancies, and various other delusions; there are plenty of occasions when people have no reason or right to be hurt, and yet react, and for such people the artist is bound to make no concessions whatsoever. It is important, I think, to consider this aspect of writing realistic stories seriously. The late Zona Gale, whenever she drew upon a person from life for a character, wanted in some way to share whatever benefit she got from the story in question, and on one occasion, writing of an old match-selling peddler (*Last Night*), and learning of his death shortly thereafter, she insisted upon erecting a memorial stone to him and spent days in searching for the place

of his burial, which she never did find, with the result that
the stone was left in the first potter's field she reached after
giving up hope of finding the old man's grave. Artistic
integrity does not rest upon the reactions of readers, however, and the writer must write as he sees fit to write. Yet
it is not impossible to avoid giving needless pain to those who
may have served in some way as models for an author's characters.

The process of creation is usually akin to physiological
digestion in that the writer is moved by a man or woman of
his acquaintance, or by a series of events, to consider them
in the light of fiction; there begins then a process of assimilation in the course of which characters and plot are grown,
all bearing the impress of the writer's own personality and
the touch of his own individual interpretation, and presently
—it may be hours after, it may be years—the story takes
shape. Most usually in the process of inner growth, the
fiction, no less realistic than life, nevertheless has such
changed aspects that character is not often identifiable with
person. But the writer should always make certain, both
from the legal and the moral perspectives, that the similarity is not too marked.

In the realistic story more than any other, the beginner
must decide for himself just how plain-spoken he is going
to be. The four-letter words, however great their integrity
in the history of our language, have been discarded because
of the prurience of thousands of small-minded people
throughout the centuries since Chaucer. The writer may
feel that, nevertheless, he cannot give the full flavor of a
character without reproducing his language to some extent.
If he is honestly convinced to this effect, then he should use

whatever language he sees fit to use, observing these general rules: avoid over-use, and in general delete from the manuscript for magazine printing, restore for book printing. The controversy about the use of "blunt" language in such a book as John Steinbeck's *The Grapes of Wrath,* for instance, almost completely obscured the meaning and timeliness of that book, both as art and as propaganda.

The use of questionable language, of course, comes in under the major head of detail-selection. So too does the inclination to describe intimate details, gruesome situations, and generally to delineate in specific detail any scene or event which is likely to give offense to large numbers of readers. Given time, the writer will learn how to work out his detail-selection problem. Given experience, he will be able to develop not only a skilled hand at detail-selection, but also a perception in regard to reflecting life without simply recording it.

A Reading List

The "Hardboiled" School

THE FIFTH COLUMN and THE FIRST FORTY-NINE STORIES, by Ernest Hemingway (1938)

FOR WHOM THE BELL TOLLS, by Ernest Hemingway (1940)

JACKPOT, by Erskine Caldwell (1940)

THE POSTMAN ALWAYS RINGS TWICE, by James M. Cain (1934)

PIPE NIGHT, by John O'Hara (1945)

FILES ON PARADE, by John O'Hara (1939)

STUDS LONIGAN, by James T. Farrell (1935)

I Can Get It For You Wholesale, by Jerome Weidman (1937)

The Horse That Could Whistle "Dixie", by Jerome Weidman (1939)

The Regional Story

Background

Old Chester Tales, by Margaret Deland (1898)

The Hoosier Schoolmaster, by Edward Eggleston (1871)

A Son of the Middle Border, by Hamlin Garland (1917)

The Luck of Roaring Camp, by Bret Harte (1870)

The Story of a Country Town, by E. W. Howe (1884)

Best Stories of Sarah Orne Jewett (1925)

Zury, by Joseph Kirkland (1877)

Wolfville Days, by Alfred Henry Lewis (1902)

The Octopus, by Frank Norris (1901)

Life on the Mississippi, by Mark Twain (1899)

Best Stories of Mary E. Wilkins-Freeman (1927)

The Log of a Cowboy, by Andy Adams (1903)

John March, Southerner, by George W. Cable (1899)

Uncle 'Lisha's Shop, by Rowland Robinson (1897)

Winesburg, Ohio, by Sherwood Anderson (1919)

Tar, by Sherwood Anderson (1927)

Sister Carrie, by Theodore Dreiser (1901-7)

Jennie Gerhardt, by Theodore Dreiser (1911)

Moon Calf, by Floyd Dell (1920)

O Pioneers!, by Willa Cather (1913)

My Antonia, by Willa Cather (1918)

Hillsboro People, by Dorothy Canfield (1915)

Birth, by Zona Gale (1918)

Main Street, by Sinclair Lewis (1920)

BABBITT, by Sinclair Lewis (1922)
SKEETERS KIRBY, by Edgar Lee Masters (1923)
MITCH MILLER, by Edgar Lee Masters (1920)
THE MAGNIFICENT AMBERSONS, by Booth Tarkington (1918)
ETHAN FROME, by Edith Wharton (1911)

Contemporary: The Midwest

DWELL IN THE WILDERNESS, by Alvah C. Bessie (1935)
THE FARM, by Louis Bromfield (1933)
THREE MILES SQUARE, by Paul Corey (1939)
COUNTRY GROWTH, by August Derleth (1940)
U. S. A., by John dos Passos (1938)
SHOW BOAT, by Edna Ferber (1926)
SO BIG, by Edna Ferber (1924)
THE GREEN BUSH, by John T. Frederick (1925)
THE LOON FEATHER, by Iola Fuller (1940)
YOUR LIFE LIES BEFORE YOU, by Harry Hansen (1935)
REMEMBER THE DAY, by Kenneth Horan (1937)
NOW IN NOVEMBER, by Josephine Johnson (1934)
THE VOICE OF BUGLE ANN, by MacKinlay Kantor (1936)
FREE LAND, by Rose Wilder Lane (1938)
THE INVASION, by Janet Lewis (1932)
MILLBROOK, by Della T. Lutes (1938)
THREE STEEPLES, by Leroy MacLeod (1931)
THE ROOFS OF ELM STREET, by William McNally (1936)
GIANTS IN THE EARTH, by Ole E. Rolvaag (1927)
AMERICAN YEARS, by Harold Sinclair (1938)
REMEMBERING LAUGHTER, by Wallace Stegner (1937)
STATE FAIR, by Phil Stong (1932)

COUNTRY PEOPLE, by Ruth Suckow (1924)
THE ODYSSEY OF A NICE GIRL, by Ruth Suckow (1925)
THE GRANDMOTHERS, by Glenway Wescott (1927)
KING'S ROW, by Henry Bellamann (1940)
THE TREES, by Conrad Richter (1940)
JOURNEY IN THE DARK, by Martin Flavin (1943)

Contemporary: New England

VOICES IN THE SQUARE, by George Abbe (1938)
A MIGHTY FORTRESS, by LeGrand Cannon, Jr. (1937)
AS THE EARTH TURNS, by Gladys Hasty Carroll (1933)
HERE I STAY, by Elizabeth Coatsworth (1938)
LOST PARADISE, by Robert P. Tristram Coffin (1931)
THE LAST ADAM, by James Gould Cozzens (1933)
LIFE WITH FATHER, by Clarence Day (1935)
ROME HAUL, by Walter D. Edmonds (1929)
MOSTLY CANALLERS, by Walter D. Edmonds (1934)
HEMPFIELD, by David Grayson (1915)
THEY SELDOM SPEAK, by Leland Hall (1936)
THE BRIGHT SHAWL, by Joseph Hergesheimer (1922)
THE THREE BLACK PENNYS, by Joseph Hergesheimer
   (1917)
ANOTHER OPHELIA, by Edwin Lanham (1938)
THE LONG VIEW, by Hilda Morris (1937)
THE GOVERNOR OF MASSACHUSETTS, by Elliot Paul (1930)
AUTUMN, by Robert Nathan (1921)
THE ROLLING YEARS, by Agnes Sligh Turnbull (1936)
THE RUNNING OF THE DEER, by Dan Wickenden (1938)
OUR TOWN, by Thornton Wilder (1938)
COME SPRING, by Ben Ames Williams (1940)

WHITE MULE, by William Carlos Williams (1937)
LIFE ALONG THE PASSAIC RIVER, by William Carlos Williams
    (1938)

Contemporary: The Border States

FISH ON THE STEEPLE, by Ed Bell (1935)
MANY THOUSANDS GONE, by John Peale Bishop (1931)
BARREN GROUND, by Ellen Glasgow (1925)
PENHALLY, by Caroline Gordon (1931)
ALECK MAURY, SPORTSMAN, by Caroline Gordon (1934)
THE LAUGHING PIONEER, by Paul Green (1932)
THE LONG NIGHT, by Andrew Nelson Lytle (1936)
THE TIME OF MAN, by Elizabeth Madox Roberts (1926)
RIVER OF EARTH, by James Still (1940)
THE STORE, by T. S. Stribling (1932)
HEAD O' W-HOLLOW, by Jesse Stuart (1936)
MEN OF THE MOUNTAINS, by Jesse Stuart (1941)
THE TRAIPSIN' WOMAN, by Jean Thomas (1931)
NIGHT RIDER, by Robert Penn Warren (1938)

Contemporary: The South

CINNAMON SEED, by Hamilton Basso (1934)
THE HANDSOME ROAD, by Gwen Bristow (1938)
STEAMBOAT ROUND THE BEND, by Ben Lucien Burman
    (1935)
TOBACCO ROAD, by Erskine Caldwell (1932)
LIGHT IN AUGUST, by William Faulkner (1932)
THE SOUND AND THE FURY, by William Faulkner (1929)
THIS BODY THE EARTH, by Paul Green (1935)
PURSLANE, by Bernice Kelly Harris (1939)
THE FOXES, by R. P. Harriss (1936)

RETURN NOT AGAIN, by Annette Heard (1937)
MAMBA'S DAUGHTERS, by DuBose Heyward (1929)
POINT NOIR, by Clelie Benton Huggins (1937)
THE KEEPERS OF THE HOUSE, by Harry Harrison Kroll (1940)
THE LOOKING GLASS, by William March (1943)
LAMB IN HIS BOSOM, by Caroline Miller (1933)
GREEN MARGINS, by E. P. O'Donnell (1936)
BLACK APRIL, by Julia Peterkin (1927)
SOUTH MOON UNDER, by Marjorie Kinnan Rawlings (1933)
THE YEARLING, by Marjorie Kinnan Rawlings (1938)
LOOK AWAY!, by James Street (1936)
A RIVER GOES WITH HEAVEN, by Howell Vines (1930)
LOOK HOMEWARD, ANGEL, by Thomas Wolfe (1929)
FROM DEATH TO MORNING, by Thomas Wolfe (1934)
UNCLE TOM'S CHILDREN, by Richard Wright (1938)
SO RED THE ROSE, by Stark Young (1935)

Contemporary: West of the Mississippi

LONG FURROWS, by Dora Aydelotte (1935)
DEATH COMES FOR THE ARCHBISHOP, by Willa Cather (1927)
A PRAYER FOR TOMORROW, by J. Hyatt Downing (1938)
FIGURES IN A LANDSCAPE, by Paul Horgan (1940)
SPRING STORM, by Alvin Johnson (1936)
THE UNWILLING JOURNEY, by C. P. Lee (1940)
OKLAHOMA TOWN, by George Milburn (1931)
THE HOME PLACE, by Dorothy Thomas (1936)
WHAT PEOPLE SAID, by W. L. White (1938)
MY OWN, MY NATIVE LAND, by Thyra Samter Winslow (1935)

FOLK-SAY, ed. by B. A. Botkin (1929, 1930, 1931, 1932)
MAIN LINE WEST, by Paul Horgan (1936)
LAUGHING BOY, by Oliver La Farge (1929)
FLOWERING JUDAS, by Katherine Anne Porter (1931)
THE SEA OF GRASS, by Conrad Richter (1937)
OLD JULES, by Mari Sandoz (1935)
A CURTAIN OF GREEN, by Eudora Welty (1940)
THE WIDE NET, by Eudora Welty (1943)
THE LAND IS BRIGHT, by Archie Binns (1939)
BITTER CREEK, by James Boyd (1939)
HONEY IN THE HORN, by H. L. Davis (1935)
CHILDREN OF GOD, by Vardis Fisher (1939)
THE GRAPES OF WRATH, by John Steinbeck (1939)
TORTILLA FLAT, by John Steinbeck (1935)
THE LONG RIFLE, by Stewart Edward White (1932)
HOLD AUTUMN IN YOUR HAND, by George Sessions Perry
     (1941)

The Elliptic Story

SHORT STORIES FROM THE NEW YORKER (1940)
O. HENRY MEMORIAL AWARD PRIZE STORIES—of 1941, 1942,
     1943, 1944, 1945.
BEST SHORT STORIES—of 1941, 1942, 1943, 1944, 1945.
THE HERMIT PLACE, by Mark Schorer (1941)
THE PILGRIM HAWK, by Glenway Wescott (1942)
THE STATE OF MIND, by Mark Schorer (1946)

II: THE ROMANTIC STORY

A romance, according to the *Concise Oxford Dictionary,* is a "prose tale with scene and incidents remote from everyday life," or a "set of facts, episode, love affair, &c., suggesting such tales by its strangeness or moving nature." A romancer, according to the same source, is a "fantastic liar." Considerably more than nine out of ten average readers would identify a "romance" as a love story, and, while virtually everything in prose fiction not manifestly realistic (and some realistic prose as well) is romance, the fact is that a majority of the stories published in the slick-paper, confession, and pulp magazines are love stories of one kind or another.

Though the western story, the detective story, and various other type stories are no less romantic stories, the emphasis is on love in a majority of our slick-paper and pulp magazines. But in one aspect, the dictionary definition is no longer to be completely accepted; the set of facts of the tale of romance in our day is not any more so very "remote from everyday life" as the dictionary would have us believe. There is good reason for this, of course. As the literacy of a population increases, readers tend to reject the too impossible. If we accept the psychologists' decision that the compulsion to read romance fiction arises from a certain desire to compensate for a lack of what the readers feel is genuine romance in their own lives, it is understandable enough that readers should demand at least the frame of reality for their romances. The days of reader-identification with princes on horseback and princesses in towers are gone; the average reader of today finds it far more credible to think of himself or herself in terms of a recognizable symbol of American life—the actress, the businessman or woman, the factory worker, the commuter, etc., etc. The tremendous success of the confession magazines and the contemporary growth of such magazines as *True Story* and *Real Story* bear testimony to that fact.

All romance-reading tends to be in the nature of wish-fulfillment or reader-identification with the hero. It has been said with some sound analysis that men and boys like Mark Twain's *Adventures of Tom Sawyer* and *Huck Finn* because these stories are idealizations of boy-life such as they "might have had" if circumstances had been kinder, or might actually yet enjoy, in the case of boys. The hard-working house-wife who listens to the daily soap operas certainly identifies herself with the heroine—she shares her pleasure, her tribulations, and her romance, though she is usually left more satisfied than ever with her lot, for the tribulations of the average soap heroine are many and great indeed. Identification with such characters may be so complete as to convince the reader or listener of their actual reality. I remember on one occasion overhearing a voluble conversation going on in a room adjoining one in which I worked, between my great-aunt and another woman, about a certain lady who had been hospitalized, and about whose coming operation my great-aunt was expressing unmistakably genuine concern; judge my astonishment to discover that the unfortunate lady was the heroine of a soap opera! Just so have readers accepted the reality of characters in romantic stories, as the classic case of Sherlock Holmes affords ample evidence, Sir Arthur Conan Doyle having been deluged for most of his life since Holmes made his initial appearance with requests directed to Holmes to come along and solve crimes, etc.

The writer must therefore take such self-identification and escape motives into consideration. And he must do so with an eye for his specific market, if he is slanting his story. To the average reader of the confession magazines, for instance, the stories almost always ring true. This is simply because the characters, the circumstances of the stories, the environment are all within the often limited boundaries of the reader. The fundamental theme is common human experience—I sinned and I paid; where it enters into the sphere of wish-fulfillment is in its most usually happy ending, after sinning and paying, the bill having been paid, the characters presumably live in contentment, a lesson learned, for the rest of their natural lives. The fact that such an ultimate denouement very seldom takes place in life does not diminish the enjoyment of the reader; it is enough to reflect that, however improbable, such an ending *might* take place, it is not beyond possibility, and therefore, it *seems* real, in exactly the way it seems to readers a genuine, if second-hand, experience to live the life of the character of a story while it is being read. There, too, the dominating rationalization of the reader is primarily this— that in another set of circumstances directing his own life, the romance might have been his own biography.

Given the fundamental themes of sinning and paying, of love, conflict, and victory, of crime and punishment, etc., the setting makes very little difference. The ultimate course of a romantic story is always eminently predictable, whether it is set in Nome or in Timbuctoo, in Gopher Prairie or in Medicine Hat, in London or Calcutta. A love story can proceed just as inevitably to its destined conclusion in a railway train traveling from Cincinnati to Chicago as in the glamor of Shepheard's Hotel, in Cairo. The common denominator remains the measure of individual experience, and this is something the aspiring writer must never forget.

The romantic story is always the most orthodox of all stories to plot. It is almost without exception charted as aspiration, conflict, achievement. It might be said of the realistic story, on the other hand, that it may be either aspiration, conflict, conditional achievement or aspiration, conflict, defeat. This is as true of the detective story as of the adventure story, but above all, it is true of the love story, for which the widest possible market always exists. The variations in demands for that market are not insurmountable, by any means. While many slicks and all the pulp magazines featuring love stories concern themselves primarily with story, the slicks by and large do often want stronger and fuller characterizations, convincing motivations, and more skilled writing.

I confess quite frankly that, while I can do it and have done it in a comparatively short time, the writing of a straightforward love story with emphasis purely on story, is a trying chore. I personally prefer a story with those qualities demanded by most of the slick-paper magazines, particularly those which are not too insistent on rigid adherence to traditional formulae. A story of this kind does require a little more insight into the conditions of human experience, as this in turn demands closer observation of life, more study, and a somewhat extended skill in interpretation which are not

...eeded in anything remotely like so great a degree by the romancer in the pulp division. Stories in this tradition are usually founded on some kind of fact a little more obviously than formulae stories, which are founded rather on possible conditions of fact and experience.

Working techniques vary widely, but it may be instructive to examine the genesis of what is perhaps my best-liked "romance", the novelette, *Any Day Now*, originally published in *Redbook* for May, 1938, subsequently in a limited edition in book form, and finally in my short story collection, *Country Growth* (Scribner's, 1940). This is the story of an extremely attractive young woman who said "No" when she should have said "Yes" and did not marry at all, as a result —an unusual story apart from formula in that its ending was not "happy" though it was not realistic, either. It, and other such stories, have their inception in real life and real people, and *Any Day Now* began with the sight, literally, of an old photograph. It was the photograph of a sixteen-year-old girl who was breathtakingly beautiful, and I realized with considerable surprise that I knew the original, then a woman in her early fifties.

Writers, no less than other people, may fall into the major error of taking their surroundings and their neighbors for granted. I had known the original of the photograph for years: a heavy-set, fiftyish woman, garrulous, single—not an "old maid" by any means—demonstrative, talkative (and repetitive), good-looking still, but restless with that restlessness common to all people when the landmarks of youth begin to recede with the passing of time. There had always been vague, careless talk of her going with some man here or there —she worked in the city and came out to Sac Prairie for her vacations, as she had always done since her parents' death —talk in the manner of small towns, not malicious, not concerned, simply talk; but now, at sight of the old photograph, I asked myself for the first time why a girl as striking as she had been had never been married. And, having asked myself this, I was shortly convinced that in its answer there lay a story.

I began therefore to dig around among the friends of her own age and older and unearthed the assorted trivia of fact and fiction which inevitably accumulate about every life, wherever it is lived. The essential answer to my question ultimately emerged when an older woman remembered that "She was always the same to all the men. She was as popular as can be, but she treated them all wonderfully. There were probably a lot of men in love with her. I don't think any of us realized just how they felt until one day when I was coming home on the train. I was sitting in the daycoach just a few miles out of town, and just behind me two traveling salesmen were talking—comparing notes, you might say. It turned out that each one of them had a ring in his pocket, and each one meant to ask his girl to become his wife. Naturally, going to the same town, they began to talk about the girls, and it turned out that both of them were thinking of Renna. That was the way she was. Neither one then asked her."

But that, however fascinating it was, did not suit my purpose for a story of romance. Her popularity was good, yes —the young men, "the steady and the wild together around her like hawkmoths hovered about the roadside phlox in the summer dusk"—but an adequate delineation of her treating all the young men with the same disarming and deceptive friendliness would take far too much space to make convincing than I felt the story was worth. I elected instead to take up the story of her liking for a village doctor, reverse the roles, establish the doctor as the most popular of the men around her, and create in her mother the conflict which actually existed within herself. Her mother became a symbol, opposing the struggling young doctor, aware of her daughter's beauty to such an extent that she was convinced Renna might do better than the doctor, and I utilized the weakness which (if weakness it was) had prevented her from making a choice among her beaux by causing her to give ear to her mother's insistence, so that when the doctor proposed, she rejected him, only to find subsequently that she loved him; but her determination to tell him so was given no opportunity, he married someone else, and she was suddenly bereft of the man she loved above all others. In this, then, I had my story. I opened it with a prefatory scene in the present, and drew the reader back into the past, from the woman of fifty to the young woman she had been, and from there took him up the years into the present once more.

This then is a typical romantic story which grew out of life. Better than half of it was completely real; the rest was imaginative. But the realistic portion was little more than setting and character—what was imagined held the kernel and action of the story. In such proportions more than one of the stories appearing in the slick-paper magazines are created.

The plots and characters which give rise to such stories are always present, and the novice has only to exercise his choice. Getting at them goes back to the need for constant vigilance in observation. It is an old truism that there is at least one story in every life; the writer must find it and write it. In searching for it, he will be surprised at how often the themes of the most commonplace formulae in romantic fiction crop up to be recognized. And he will be surprised furthermore by the infinite variations and refinements offered. A long time ago I resolved some day to write a novelette about the theme of what I call "the millstone mother"—that is, the selfish woman who prevents her daughter or son from getting married because she wants her for herself.

The theme is "as old as the hills," to quote a colloquial expression common in Wisconsin. I had known two such cases, both rather flagrant. Both were mothers who kept a tight rein on their daughters. The mothers were in each case well up in their sixties, and the daughters were approaching forty. In both cases, the mothers were wealthy. I did not have occasion to meet them often, but I lost no opportunity to study the mothers—candidly, I was not particularly interested in the daughters who, though in both cases very good-looking, I dismissed as singularly weak to permit themselves to be so imposed upon; and I formed the opinion that both old women were inordinately vain and selfish and would stop at absolutely nothing to achieve their end, insofar as their daughters were concerned. Having arrived at this conclusion, I soon unearthed plenty of facts to warrant its justification; and with this in mind I ultimately wrote the story, *The Night Light at Vorden's* (*Redbook*, September, 1942).

I drew upon fact only for the basic ruse employed by both old women—whenever a suitor became too pressing and their daughters began to weaken, the old women took them on long trips abroad and simply kept them there until the suitor's ardor cooled and his attentions turned elsewhere, and I elected to write my story from the point-of-view of the girl's "last" chance which occurred at a time when financial losses made such an escaping trip impossible. I had therefore, an interesting experience which highlights the sometimes marked differences of opinion which exist between editor and author. In this case the editor was Edwin Balmer, one of the most competent and liberal-minded of all editors with whom I have dealt, and himself an author of by no means small stature, and the difference of opinion resolved about the methods I had the old woman utilize to frighten away the suitor and keep her daughter by her.

These methods were, I felt, not at all impossible, judged by what I knew of the women whom I had had under observation. Faced with the fact that her daughter had fallen in love with the new high school principal in Sac Prairie, Mrs. Vorden did, successively, three things to ruin her chances—first, she suggested to the Board of Education that the principal was making undesirable advances to her daughter; secondly, failing in her first attempt, she wrote to the principal himself an anonymous note warning him that his sweetheart was very likely to become insane, since there was insanity in the Vorden family; and finally, she carefully staged a melodramatic attempt to set the house afire, being meticulous about making it not only possible but inevitable that her daughter should discover and put out the fire and save her mother from her grief in time to prevent any but superficial damage from being done. The

final attempt was deliberately designed to open the girl's
eyes, for, though her suitor was well aware of what was
going on, he could not openly oppose her mother, lest, by
dividing the girl's loyalties, he accomplish the very separa-
tion the old woman sought.

Mr. Balmer accepted the first method without a qualm;
this he felt might be quite in character. But he balked at the
second and third; he could not believe that any mother
would actually be guilty of utilizing such means to gain her
end. I was willing to stake what small professional reputation I had that such a woman as Mrs. Vorden would do
just those things, and perhaps even more I had not had the
temerity to chronicle. Editor and author were thus at an
impasse; Mr. Balmer wanted the story, but he wanted
changes made. I felt that to make all the changes he asked
would weaken the story to a point where it would become
simply incredible in that no adequate awakening would
have been brought to the girl sufficient to cause her to take
matters into her own hands and defy her mother by going
away with her suitor to be married. We had, therefore, to
effect a compromise; I eliminated the final fire, and substi-
tuted a more obvious method—having Mrs. Vorden simply
remove her daughter's clothing from her closet and lock
her into her room—and retained the anonymous note. In
this form the story was published. Within four days of its
appearance in *Redbook* I had a letter from an unknown
woman in New Jersey, stating that *The Night Light at
Vorden's,* with certain changes, might have been the story
of her life—and to prove it, she enclosed a letter her mother
had written to her suitor, now her husband for two decades
or more. With but one difference, that letter was the same

save for word alterations, as the fictitious letter of Mrs. Vorden; the major difference was that in my correspondent's case, her mother had signed the letter, and had not sent it anonymously!

It is obviously not often that an author's conclusions based on observation of people intended as bases for characters in fiction are so promptly corroborated. I was no less surprised at this corroboration than Mr. Balmer. Editors may be in error, but I think the aspiring writer is wise to act on the principle that by and large, in the great majority of cases, the editor is right. The writer has but one really legitimate quarrel with editors as a whole; he can present a very good case for more real reader guidance by editors, instead of permitting reader taste averages to be imposed upon a magazine from cover to cover; and yet this is distinctly outside the province of the writer to contend, since the responsibility is the editor's, and not that of his writers.

The beginner in writing is often all too likely to regard what he has written as sacred. It requires a great deal of experience to effect that adjustment necessary to a balanced perspective on editorial requests for changes or outright changes made in editorial offices with or without consent of the author. Sometimes the metamorphosis of a story can be extremely enlightening. Consider such a story as *McCrary's Wife*, for instance, which appeared in *Good Housekeeping* for August, 1944. *McCrary's Wife* had its inception on a trip to New York, when, in the company of a friend's wife and child en route to Philadelphia, the three of us were mistaken by the conductor on the Chicago-Fort Wayne run for a family, and given a great many intimate details of the conductor's own life. He was now a grandfather, and he was very proud of his grandchildren; he took such pleasure in telling us about his family that neither of us had the heart to tell him we were not a family. Two or three times on his run he stopped at our seats and talked. I might have forgotten this incident had it not been for the fact that, on my return trip alone a fortnight later, the conductor coming on at Fort Wayne for the run back to Chicago, paused at my seat and inquired after my "wife". It was on the tip of my tongue to tell him he had made a mistake when I thought better of it; I said only that she was visiting her folks, and thereafter, till I reached Chicago, I was regaled with the most recent trivia of the conductor's family life. It occurred to me at that moment that, given a lonely young man in his thirties or circa forty, he might easily fall into the fantasy of regarding his friend's attractive wife as his own, a fiction which the conductor would willy-nilly keep alive. If then, he became inured to this fantasy, and the conductor should suddenly be taken out of his world, his house of fiction would collapse.

I wrote the story. McCrary, of course, had no wife at all; but the conductor gave his fantasy such a reality that he began to make special trips to New York solely for the pleasure of indulging a dream which, in a way he did not understand, somehow compensated him for a little while for a lack he felt very acutely. After having established McCrary in his fantasy with his unreal wife, I had the conductor drop dead of a heart attack, and McCrary accordingly desolated by the collapse of his world, and, snapping back to reality, wondering what had happened to him. It was, manifestly, an off-trail story, but it was one not easily forgotten by editors who had seen it, with the result that it was ultimately published. How-

:ver, the ending occasioned some difficulty. As first written, :he ending, which takes place at the conclusion of that busi- :ess trip to New York on which McCrary learns of the con- luctor's death, went like this:

> The interminable trip passed, his business in New York was concluded, McCrary came down to the station to go back. Time had gone, time was lost, time had passed; his grief was assuaged a little, he had begun to adjust himself to the conductor's death, but when he came into the familiar station, when he began to realize that he had nothing at Fort Wayne to which to look forward, he was obsessed with a horror of returning on the *General,* a sudden onslaught of self-pity. He could not do it; he realized that he must cash in his return ticket, go back on some other train; it was beyond him ever again to go on that train from Fort Wayne to Chicago without the warm friendliness of the old conductor to anticipate. What shall I tell them? he thought, moving toward the window. What but the truth?
>
> "I'm sorry," he said, "I've got to cash in my ticket. My wife's died." He was grave, a little sad. "McCrary's wife," he added absently.
>
> He took his money and hurried out of the station, hailing a taxi. "New York Central," he said. "Hurry."
>
> There he sat, unmindful of the world beyond the taxi's windows, slouched in a corner of the back seat, his eyes downcast and little beads of perspiration edging his forehead. Thinking of the year and a half just past he began to feel again a terrible, violent grief, he began to give way to harsh, tearless sobs, but in a few moments he sat up, looking around a little dazedly. *What happened to me?* he asked himself. *What happened to me?* And he looked back down the traffic-filled street, as if to find somewhere there the moment gone just beyond his reach, the chance-discarded moment he had tried to

touch, to bring back out of the past, to change, the trivial, half-forgotten moment, for loss of which men die in
spirit a little at a time, unaware, unknowing how things
might have been.

He got out of the taxi at the station and went down
to get his ticket: a decorous business man, moving
steadily toward middle age: still wondering, still a little
sad, weighed down by loneliness again, the age-old loneliness of the man who knows too little affection, still asking himself, *What happened to me?*

Reading the manuscript, Miss Geraldine Rhoads of *Life
Story* felt that I erred grievously in not indicating that there
was hope for McCrary to make his fiction into a substitute
reality. I then added three paragraphs to the original ending and sent it to *Good Housekeeping,* as follows:

But as he walked along, he caught sight of himself
suddenly in a mirror, and he came to a stop. It was not
the face of an old man looking out at him; it was
scarcely that of a middle-aged man—hardly a line,
hardly a crease; and quite abruptly, quite absurdly, with
a curious sense of shy discovery, it was born in upon
him that he was far from old, he still had time. That
image of his imagined wife had died with the conductor
whose passing had taken away her reality. But surely
somewhere ahead of him, around a corner of time still
to be passed, someone waited for his coming, a woman
who might understand his loneliness, who might indeed
some day become McCrary's wife!

The suddenness of the thought intoxicated him.

He moved forward once more, his pulse beating a little
faster now, and a smile touched his lips. His eyes grew
alert once more, and he walked with a new spring in his

step, hurrying like a man, who, without other evidence than the knowledge deep within, has a rendezvous with the woman of his heart's choice—at a place and time to be inevitably disclosed to him by days and hours he hastened now to meet.

In publishing the story, however, the editors of *Good Housekeeping* decided that neither ending would do; they accordingly did not permit the conductor's death; they simply retired him and helped McCrary to keep up his fantasy by writing the conductor about his "wife" Christine and their children; so that as published, the ending came out like this:

He walked to the platform with the old conductor. They shook hands. The old man began to speak, changed his mind, turned and walked slowly along the worn and splintered boards. McCrary watched him, and he felt as though he were choking.

"Goodbye, Old Man," he whispered.

And then there was the whistle signal, and McCrary stepped back on the train. It was moving. It was going east. There were hours ahead—hours, days, years. Mc-Crary settled back in his seat. He brushed his hand across his eyes. He leaned forward then, and from his suitcase he took some paper. He found a clean sheet, smoothed it, rested it on a book, dug in his pocket for a pencil, and began to write.

"Dear John," he wrote. "We didn't have much chance for talking today, and there are lots of things I had to tell you. First of all, Christine sent you her love. She's up and about again, after her cold, and feeling quite fit. Just this morning she was saying to me—"

McCrary paused a moment. What was it Christine

had been saying to him just this morning? Oh, yes! That was it! He smiled and resumed, "She was saying to me—"

The result of all this has been, amusingly enough, that I am left undecided myself as to whether to use the first or second ending for the ultimate reprinting of *McCrary's Wife* in my next collection of short stories. I disliked the final ending, but readers did not; since the ultimate test of a story from the editorial point-of-view is the reaction of readers, the revision was justified.

The writer soon learns to defer to the judgment of most editors, particularly in the field of magazine publishing. After all, the writer may still exercise his right to preserve his original story, without changes made at editorial suggestion, when it appears in book form. The writer is well advised to develop as soon as possible a critical eye in regard to his own work; nothing is ultimately so helpful in effecting gradual and steady improvement in the quality of his work. And the writer who is honestly determined to be his own wisest critic will find many an editor exceedingly helpful; romantic fiction is a commodity with which almost every editor has had a great deal of experience which is outside the bounds of many writers, particularly the novices, who are quite likely to fall into often grotesque errors.

Human conduct does not, after all, vary too greatly, and one of the first things any writer must learn—and particularly the writer of romantic fiction—is to avoid insistence upon anything too far from the usual or the probable. If he is writing interplanetary fiction, it is quite all right to be improbable; the reader of the story accepts that premise without question. But if he is writing romantic fiction which presumes to present life in an idealized form, then it becomes his duty to avoid the too unlikely. This is true whether or not the writer has actually known of a similar event in his own experience. It is sometimes difficult for the beginning writer to understand this, but it is a simple fact that most people reject the improbable and the unlikely. Hence, all the critical to-do about the use of coincidence in fiction. Now, as a matter of fact, some of the most outrageously improbable coincidences happen in life with such regularity that they can hardly any longer be classed as "improbable"; yet their use in fiction is still taboo. Almost every one of us knows of such coincidences, which range all the way from such common experience as a friend's telephoning you at the moment you have begun quite inexplicably to think about him, to the fortuitous appearance of persons and happening of events in matters of life and death.

But the fact remains that such coincidences are not usual; they do not form a normal and natural part of daily life, and, while some slight use of coincidence is usually overlooked in most romantic or escape fiction, coincidence still remains beyond the pale for most serious fiction, realistic or romantic. But coincidence is only one example of the unusual. The same rule applies pretty generally to any major departure from behavior patterns, for instance, to any exception to scientifically known facts—and such exceptions do exist, quite regardless of the claims of scientists—, to anything unlikely or out of character, regardless of its pertinence, save only in such kinds of stories in the reading of which the reader is manifestly conditioned to accept the unusual without question. The reader of a magazine like *Weird Tales* throws out of the window the conditions of acceptance of the fiction in *Collier's,* for instance, the moment he takes up that magazine long subtitled "a magazine of the bizarre and unusual."

If the novice at writing lacks both experience and the ability to assimilate the experience of others, he would be most wise to abandon the writing of fiction until his qualifications improve. I do not mean to suggest that it is impossible to write without experience. That particular shibboleth has long since fallen by the wayside, since it has been shown again and again that experience is not vital to a writer's work if only he has the ability to assimilate the experience of others and to appreciate his fellow human beings with sympathy and understanding. The ability to assimilate experience demands, of course, the ability also to select and interpret. Many an author and actor has said simply, in explanation of his success with his characters, "I put myself in his place, and I did what I felt he would do." That is not just a line; that is all too often the literal truth, and it is a natural result of adequate study of and sympathy with any given character.

The assimilation of experience is always fundamentally a selective process, and so, too, is its interpretation; both assimilation and interpretation depend in large degree on the potential boundaries of the writer's experience (actual and in extension), and on his ability to reason. I have known authors to deduce logically enough a behavior pattern for a character whose reactions to one set of circumstances are manifest, and then go ahead with an entirely irrational behavior pattern in reaction to another similar set of circumstances. Even though most people do at times do irrational things, it is not usual. Given an individual's reaction to any given circumstances, it is usually possible for an astute and ordinarily intelligent writer to correctly estimate his probable reactions to a great many related circumstances; in fiction, as well as in real life, characters do not often depart from what is normal for them. Hence the identification of author with character, which can be so complete that it can, amusingly enough, cause difficulties—as in the case of the time when I identified myself with a very puzzled and sorely tried character who did not know which way to turn in the problem facing her, an identification which I made so thoroughly that I found myself in precisely the same position and had to seek the help of a woman friend to achieve the readiest solution to what was essentially a woman's problem. I rather think that is going somewhat too far in the process of author-identification.

Interpretations as well as assimilation are consistently dependent upon the understanding and experience of the writer, which is to say that a writer cannot either assimilate or interpret something which is completely outside both his experience and his comprehension. Faced with something of this nature, it behooves the writer, novice or professional, to acquaint himself with its meaning, and for that purpose he should have ready to hand, either at his desk or at a nearby library, all manner of references, ranging from a comprehensive dictionary to a book on psychology.

No less than in interpretation, accuracy in observation should be the writer's goal. This is as true of romantic or imaginative fiction as it is of fiction which purports to represent life faithfully. All too often the young writer fails to check his facts; he takes things for granted and sees no good reason why he should check on facts he has already come to ac-

cept. The story of the reader who protested to the editor of
a national magazine that a certain night in 1909, described
by the author of a story in that magazine, had no moon at all,
instead of the full moon indicated in the story, is perhaps
widely known. This may seem somewhat far-fetched, but it
is a legitimate complaint, just the same. The writer is morally
bound to be accurate, and there is no essential difference
between the ascription of a moon to a moonless night in 1909
and the wanton exaggeration of the population of Podunk,
U. S., for the purpose of a story, when the correct population
of Podunk is in fact well known.

The tendency to take things for granted is common
enough, and most of us must learn by experience. Despite all
the cautions to writers to write primarily about something of
which they know either directly or indirectly, novices very
often insist on straying far afield for settings. This may very
probably be because these writers have not yet developed
sufficient perspective to understand that there is potentially
as much drama and romance in their home milieu as in any
place in the world. The danger of distant settings lies in in-
adequate knowledge. In the original version of my first published short story (*Bat's Belfry, Weird Tales,* May 1926),
which was set in the country down from London (which, for
a beginner of fifteen, seems in retrospect to be the height of
self-assurance), I introduced a pub-keeper who spoke in
Cockney dialect. Possibly due to saturation reading of Conan
Doyle, Sax Rohmer, Edgar Wallace, et al, I had somehow
conceived the impression that most of the lower classes in
England habitually dropped their h's from many words and
added them to many others where they did not belong. The
late Farnsworth Wright, then editor of *Weird Tales,* pointed

out that the Cockney dialect was limited to a bounded area within the city of London, and that it was not likely that such a speech pattern would make its appearance in the down country, or, if it did, that it would last for any length of time, since all dialects are naturally subject to change under the influence of the prevailing speech patterns. Had I checked on this simple fact before submitting the story, I would not have made the error, which now necessitated revision; but I made the mistake of taking the dialect more or less for granted—I ascribed it to a class of people rather than to a district; a little unbiased interpretation would have enlightened me even without reference to any source of information, for dialects are never a matter of class, but always of region.

A somewhat similar experience happened to me in the writing of an historical novel some years ago. The writer of historical novels is peculiarly bound to refrain from taking license with historical facts if he bases his material on actual events within a limited region. This stricture requires some elucidation, of course. Writer interpretation is not under indictment in this regard; if a character known to history is presented, the writer need not try to find out his actual conversation, etc.; all he is bound to do is keep to the character as he is known to actual history (not to legend), and to present him in no impertinent variation from that character. But the writer of historical novels, possibly enamoured of what appears to him to be the glamour of historically great names, has a difficult time resisting dragging in by the heels every character known in that time and region. There is on the face of it no great harm in so doing, but most writers fall by the wayside in forgetting that they must present that great man or woman in terms of his or her own time, and not in terms of the writer's perspective on history. In his own time, for instance, Lincoln was far more reviled than the late President Franklin Delano Roosevelt was in our time; both men were widely loved, and neither in his own time could be seen in the proper perspective of history. The writer who presents Lincoln—a favorite character, incidentally—as a "great" man other than the President of the United States, many of whose simple ways were the butt of jokes among the so-called socially elect, is simply guilty of an error in perspective which has the effect of challenging the validity of his whole book. As a general rule, the writer of historical fiction ought to introduce characters, great or small, only in the order of probability; that is to say, if an historical character was known to be in the vicinity of the setting of the novel in progress at or about the time of the story, it is perfectly permissible to introduce him; but if he was known to be at the other end of the country at the time the writer wishes to introduce him in a scene in his novel, set half a continent away, there is no valid excuse for presenting him at all.

In the historical novel in question, my problem illustrated another aspect of writing about known people. I had elected to do a fictionized biography, in effect, of a well known Wisconsin pioneer, dead almost a century, and worked with the descendants of the old man in gathering and interpreting my material, which consisted of everything from letters to obituary notices. Like all locally great men, legend ascribed to him a great many misdeeds, of which I could find no proof or record; envy, jealousy, greed, and all those common motivating factors had in his own time slandered him, and these slanders had more or less come down in one form or another through the generations. As I saw him, he was by no means without fault, but his faults were on the whole picayune. I was therefore somewhat loath to present a man who had no single error in his ways, so to speak; I thought him somewhat less a man of his time. I then learned in an offhand way from one of the descendants, with whom I worked in close harmony, that her grandfather had had an Indian or half-breed mistress and had had at least two children by her, but of course, she said, I would not need to include that in the book.

Now, since my hero lived in a time and place where few white women then existed, the taking of Indian or half-breed mistresses was quite in keeping with custom. However, the family for the sake of the character—whose real name I was using in my novel—protested that this incident should not be used. I remained adamant, but I resolved just the same, to look into the facts of the matter as thoroughly as possible. Doing so, I unearthed a most interesting fact. The two children of my hero had been baptized and their births recorded in the parish records of the Catholic church in his community, and both bore his name! Now, as any one familiar with the practices and rules of the Roman Catholic Church knows, illegitimate children are never given their father's name unless a marriage has been held. Since these children were given his name in the parish records, the hero and his half-breed mistress had unquestionably been married. Further research faded the picture of an Indian squaw and brought out that of an attractive half-breed, looking far more French than Indian.

Naturally, I was delighted at this turn of events, and proposed to utilize it. Much to my astonishment, the family urged me instead to hold to my original concept of presenting her as his mistress. Having conceived their original objection to have arisen on moral grounds, I was at a loss to understand this seeming about-face, until finally, in answer to much probing, it developed that the family feared that such presentation of such facts might cause some of the descendants of that liaison to file a claim to the ancestral estate! This, of course, was wholly improbable; the records in question had been destroyed in a fire; and the hero had in fact made a handsome settlement upon each of those children, so that no court in the land would have considered a claim of such nature. I went ahead and presented my hero as I saw him, and no complications resulted.

The incident is illustrative of the scope of the author's problems. Though he may be writing a romance, the moment he begins to utilize people who have actually lived, either under their own names or thinly disguised, he is morally and ethically bound to keep to the facts of history. Admittedly, a character disguised under another name permits an author much greater liberty in this regard, but he must still hold to the facts of history as they pertain to his time. No author would think of introducing a locomotive into a story set in the time of the French Revolution, for instance, but he might not balk at a less flagrant discrepancy between history and fiction. If he does not take care, readers will sooner or later catch him up and expose him to his editors, who publish him on the justifiable assumption that he knows whereof he writes.

Another very common problem the novice must solve is that of verisimilitude. In my beginning years, many a story

I myself thought well of, was returned by editors—particularly by Farnsworth Wright, who had a fondness for the word—because it lacked "verisimilitude," which, when I took the trouble to look it up, meant simply that the story did not convince the editor, that is, did not ring true. Quite regardless of its market, a story must be convincing in theme and presentation in order to succeed. The writer is very apt to take for granted that the reader will accept his premises and conclusions because he, the writer, knows the successive steps between them, and assumes that the reader will likewise recognize those steps.

But there is no justification whatsoever for assuming that the reader will recognize anything. In realistic fiction, it is true that the reader is seldom called upon to imagine anything; but this is directly contrary to the situation in romantic or imaginative fiction, where the imagination of the reader must be called into play. The writer must admit at the outset that there are many readers who completely lack imagination of any kind; they are simply incapable of supplying omitted details; and for those readers, the writer is bound to supply the basic necessary material for the best understanding of the story. If he does not do so, then the story, in the words of Farnsworth Wright, will "lack verisimilitude" for those readers. I do not suggest that a writer must slant his material at the lowest common denominator, but he must make concessions to the average reader, because, in direct proportion as he retreats from such concessions, he loses what is understandably enough called the "common" or "human touch".

This is as true of characters as of themes and places. Obviously, a story featuring a type character in a familiar setting with a recognizable theme has something more to offer a wider variety of people than a story featuring a strange person in an alien land with a complex and highly intellectualized theme. Such writers as Dreiser, Sinclair Lewis, Sherwood Anderson, and Edgar Lee Masters have habitually used recognizable people. The excellence of such books as Anderson's *Winesburg, Ohio,* Masters' *Spoon River Anthology,* Lewis's *Main Street* and Dreiser's *Sister Carrie* lies in the fact that the majority of the readers those books may attract are familiar with similar characters. "We have people just like that in our town," you will hear readers say. And which town or city, indeed, has not its Carol Kennicot, its Cass Timberlane, its Caroline Meeber, its George Babbitt, its Editor Wheedon, and so on? True, these works are all primarily intended as realistic fiction, but in this regard, the same general rule applies to romantic fiction.

Verisimilitude is gained sometimes far more easily by simplicity in character, theme, and setting, than in complex exposition designed to explain psychological reasons for character-actions. Thus, it is much more convincing to the average reader to say of George Babbitt that he is a small town businessman, a typical joiner, whose self-importance is greatly inflated, without much reason, and who feels that simply because he is a businessman, he can "run things" and sit in judgment on his acquaintances who are not fellow businessmen but only his customers and neighbors, than it would be to explain Babbitt as a victim of his own frustrations ever seeking to compensate himself for something he feels he lacks. Both might be quite true, but the former is far more acceptable to a far greater number of people simply because it falls within the realm of personal experience of the greatest number of potential readers.

The problem of verisimilitude is related to the wider problem of social resonance. The first requirement of a created work, whatever its form—a painted picture, piece of sculpture, a book, a symphony, etc., etc.—is that it have social resonance, which means that it must communicate or contain within it the possibility of communication. It must say something to its apprehender, that is, in terms of fiction, its reader. We are not here particularly concerned with those works which do not communicate, the prototypes of which are such pieces as the tonal experiments of Gertrude Stein, James Joyce's *Finnegan's Wake,* and various experiments of people like Tristan Tzara, which, despite the hosannahs of critics, most of whom shout hosannahs in lieu of their inability to offer any adequate meaning for the works, do not communicate except on the most esoteric planes. It may therefore be accepted that a work of writing, whether fiction or not, which is simply not to be understood except with the help of dozens of ready reference works, is rather evidence of exhibitionist tendencies on the part of the authors than of anything else, whether it is an elaborate philological potpourri like *Finnegan's Wake* or a tonal rune like Miss Stein's later work—(I do not, of course, have reference to such a fine work as *Three Lives* or such a delightful book as *The Autobiography of Alice B. Toklas*).* Many critics, who are

* Apropos Miss Stein's *Wars I Have Seen,* a recent book in her usual garbled prose: on receiving her copies of the book, she cabled her publishers, Random House, BOOK RECEIVED LOVELY PAGE LOVELY BOOK LOVELY BENNETT LOVE TO RANDOM HOUSE, whereupon the publishers sent her a check made out for "two thousand thousand dollars dol-

many times unduly severe in regard to the work of young writers, are the most gullible people on earth when it comes to works which frankly lack social resonance; they remind one of that kind of Oriental mind which is so fearful of "losing face" that it will condone suicide rather than be forthright and honest about something it does not understand in common terminology, with the result that they have been hoist by their own petard, so to speak, more than once by elaborate and hilarious hoaxes deliberately perpetrated to lay them by the heels, hoaxes upon which they bite with the monotony and regularity of a school of sunfish in a millpond.

Verisimilitude is achieved in a variety of ways—simplicity of theme, recognizability of characters, familiarity of place —and the writer need not use a great deal of elaborate prose to bring out his character and setting. Ten words will do far better than a hundred, and far more memorably. Consider the simplicity of Hemingway's opening of *The Undefeated,* quoted earlier; for the alert reader, no amount of amplification would have more effectively given the setting of that story. The casual, offhand touch is twice as effective as the direct statement, which all too often intrudes upon the course of a story. I recognize this kind of intrusion in the work of many writers, as well as in my own; I suspect that even the most professional writers are not always innocent of it, failing to knit their stories together as compactly as they might do. In the short story form, particularly, brevity is a virtue for which no substitute can be offered; in the novel, the

lars." Miss Stein cabled back CUT OUT THIS NONSENSE AND MAKE MY CHECK OUT PROPERLY. This was doubtless a severe blow to the cultists who were looking for her to wire something like this: A DOLLAR IS A DOLLAR IS A DOLLAR IS NEVER A THOUSAND DOLLARS etc.

writer obviously has more latitude and the reader expects such latitude to be taken.

Nevertheless, there are great numbers of readers who insist upon movement. The same theme treated by Kathleen Norris and Thomas Wolfe would find enthusiastic readers for the respective finished products by Norris and Wolfe at a ratio of something like a thousand to one. That is simply because Mrs. Norris would treat her theme objectively and with movement, while Wolfe would have been intensely subjective, and movement would be only incidental. Very often, too, readers divide with no semblance of logic; one reader will write that he has much enjoyed the "wonderful descriptive passages", and will add that he did not, however, care much for the story; while another will write that he enjoyed the story tremendously, he thought it was presented with "fine insight," but the "descriptive passages, in my opinion, greatly retarded its movement." These are, perhaps, manifest differences in taste, and one cannot argue about matters of taste, since no one knows precisely what factors, environmental and hereditary, have gone into the formation of individual tastes.

The division between proponents of the objective method and those of the subjective method has a certain superficial parallel in the constant issues between readers of fast action mysteries on the one hand and those who are devotees of the deductive school on the other. Both types of stories are usually objective, but there is a similarity in the issue as concerns movement, because the deductive story is primarily one which appeals to the intellect, while the action detective story has its primary appeal to lovers of adventure. It is only rarely, as in the case of such an assured stylist as Raymond Chandler, that readers of mystery stories from both schools of thought are unanimous in approval. By and large, the lovers of Sherlock Holmes, Fr. Brown, Dr. Thorndyke, *et al.*, do not care a great deal for Sam Spade and his followers, and vice versa.

Movement in a story is a primary factor in the difference, technically, between the objective narrative and the subjective. The former can be slow in movement, the latter can be fast; but as a general rule, it is the other way around— the objective story moves rather more quickly than the subjective. Of more importance to the writer, however, is method; the objective story is purely external to the mind, and is seldom distinguished by any attempt on the part of the writer to interpret, whereas the subjective is just the opposite, the interpreted story, very often psychological and opinionated in the literary sense. Thus, the work of such writers as Zane Grey, William McLeod Raine, B. M. Bower, etc., the majority of the work of Faith Baldwin, Kathleen Norris, Ruby Ayres, Maysie Grieg, etc., almost all detective, Western, and general adventure stories are objective in treatment, while the work of such writers as the regionalists usually is not. The elliptic story has the appearance of objectivity, but it is subtly subjective. The objective story requires fully as much observation and detail-selection as the subjective story, and in some cases, paradoxical as it may seem, it is more difficult to make convincing than a subjective story, because the objective story writer must depend upon purely external aspects of character and setting to convince his reader, while the subjective story's author can fall back upon a sound psychological interpretation which affords the reader no loophole for doubt.

There is no such thing as a difference in author ability insofar as the two kinds of stories are written; the objective story, which may seem easier to write—and certainly is for some writers—is no less difficult than the subjective story. Each writer obviously must write what he can do best; if he is by nature a questioning, curious individual, chances are that he will not himself be convinced by the purely external trappings of the objective story, and will sooner or later turn to the subjective method in order to restore his own faith in himself and his work. I have written both, but have myself a marked preference for the latter, that is, the subjective method, because I am difficult to convince in the objective alone.

Moreover, the problem of detail selection remains, no matter what one writes. Just how much of character or setting to include in a story is a major issue for many beginners. As a general rule, the author must be his own guide; he must include as much of description as he feels is necessary to the portrayal of his character or setting, but he should do his best to prevent such description from intruding too much. Whether a writer is creating in the objective or the subjective, he must himself remain as objective as possible while he is writing; if he fails to remain objective, he inevitably comes up against the difficulty of under-delineation, the flaw of taking for granted that the reader will readily imagine what is manifest to the writer. And, in order to be at his best, no matter what he writes, the author should fully realize his characters and setting before he puts them on paper.

A character seldom springs full-blown to life. He may— techniques of what is loosely called "inspiration" and of writing vary greatly, and it is folly to attempt a series of hard and fast rules, since virtually every rule has been defied with impunity by writers—but the beginner had better not count on his doing so. He evolves slowly. He may be a combination of people known in real life. My bucolic character, Gus Elker, is grown from at least three country people of my acquaintance, for instance, while his fellow conspirators, Great-Uncle Joe Stoll and Great-Aunt Lou, are an extension from the life. The evolving of a character is often a slow and sometimes painful process, and an author grows with his character, and ultimately, for the period of his creation, he becomes his character—and it is during this period that it is most difficult for the novice at writing to maintain an artistic objectivity in his work.

If a character is not fully grown in his creator's mind, the writer may be caught up for annoying inconsistencies. In this regard, the novice may experience his greatest danger in the writing of anything based on his own experiences, for he is likely to take his own experience so much for granted that, unless he mirrors it faithfully in his writing, he is very likely to overlook such superficial changes as he has made. An amusing example of this occurred in my own autobiographical novel, *Evening in Spring*. Opening chapter six is a brief scene between the "I" of the novel and his sweetheart's father, who warns him away from his daughter. This scene was taken from life in toto; it had happened one morning on my way to high school. For the purpose of my novel, I had set the scene at noontime, and the chapter begins thusly: "It was a day in early December that I came out of the house at noon on my way to school and knew that I was going to meet Margery's father on his way to work." Shortly after I had begun this scene, I left my typewriter to hurry to the University of Wisconsin for a lecture I had to give to a class in regional literature. When I came back, I resumed where I had left off—with this difference: I slipped into the life completely, forgetting the fictional alterations, so that, two pages further on, the surprised reader finds the continuation of the scene, after the boy has reached school, going like this: "Miss Ennis was in charge of the assembly this morning period." The transition from fiction to life was so easily and readily made, that this discrepancy slipped by me in galleys and page proofs, and was not noticed until the finished book was in my hands when, a year later, I took occasion to go through it once more!

This was in good part the result of haste. Now, there is nothing to be gained by rushing to get a character down on paper. There is certainly no harm—rather the opposite—in chronicling portions of character concepts as they occur and grow, but no attempt ought to be made to delineate the complete character until the writer is himself completely acquainted with his creation. Character presentation is fundamentally as important to a romantic story as to a realistic story, though the latter does very often call for a more complete development, sometimes on several planes.

Allied to the problem of verisimilitude is that of motivation.

In the vast majority of romantic stories, short and long, the motivation is love. As perhaps the most powerful drive and urge in mankind, love is the most readily accepted motivation for any story and any happening in the story. So powerful is the love motivation in human existence that the average reader is quite ready to believe in everything from crimes of passion and suicide on the one hand, to abject immolation and grotesque exhibitionism on the other, when love is the motive. It would seem therefore that because of the ready acceptance of this all-powerful motive, the writer might be able to underscore his motive at the expense of verisimilitude.

Unfortunately, this is not true. However universal as an emotion, love, too, remains consistent in its direction, and love as a subject requires far more understanding and experience (or assimilated experience) than any other emotion. The variations and complexities of love are innumerable. I discovered the pattern with memorable impact during the writing of *Wind Over Wisconsin*, which was written on the theme of idealism versus materialism and the need for compromise. My young protagonist, Chalfonte Pierneau, having conceived a parallel between his idealism and the stubborn and just struggle of the Sac Indian chieftain, Black Hawk, against the predatory white settlers allied himself to the Sac cause. Just or unjust, history called for the defeat of the Sac cause and no improvement in the rapacious methods of the fur traders, so opposed by Pierneau in his idealism. It was my intention to utilize this defeat of Black Hawk and the Indian's ready acceptance of the white man's victory personally as well as tribally, to force compromise upon the idealistic Pierneau. But I had forgotten one vital factor: Chalfonte's wife. She had been portrayed as a woman who loved her husband deeply, and it struck me as a simple fact that any woman so in love with her husband would sustain him in his idealism even if she herself disagreed with him, and, as long as such an incurable idealist as Pierneau had a single person to lean upon, his conversion to compromise would be all but impossible. The only solution was the originally unplanned death of Chalfonte's wife. This was an aspect of the love motivation in the novel about which I had not thought at the time I had planned the novel.

As the universality of love is beyond question, it is understandable enough that it should be not only the most potent motivation, but also the most acceptable to the reader. In one form or another, the love story has more readers than any other type of story, and a startling majority of all fiction concerns itself with love. But the writer of love stories soon finds that not only does love as a motivation have a fairly consistent pattern, but that virtually all his markets have surprisingly specific formulae to which the hopeful contributor must adhere. In addition to the formulae, there are the taboos —more of them concerned with love than any other. By and large, in American magazines there is no sinning followed by happiness or lack of punishment. One of my best short novels never appeared in a magazine simply because the characters enjoyed eight years of adulterous happiness before retribution overtook them.

Now, in the light of American life as it is a) lived to the knowledge of any alert person; b) chronicled in the newspapers; c) recorded by court clerks, etc., etc., these strictures are actually the height of absurdity. But, in effect, they are the pointing up of idealized romance; they are themselves as romantic a fiction as anything by Kathleen Norris, in whose books divorce is abhorred, for instance. Nevertheless, the taboos are there; the author must learn to cope with them, and the easiest way to do so is to shape his story to that end from the beginning. I have made unwelcome changes in stories for magazine publication; I have made changes which actually weakened the entire motivation of a story to the point of the grotesque; but these changes were demanded as a condition of acceptance, and I duly eliminated them in favor of the story as originally written in every case for book publication.

Such changes might be said to represent the artist's concession to the writer.

Somewhere along the way the writer must decide whether he is a creative artist, a professional writer, or both. If he attempts to be both, he will sooner or later come face to face with a popular belief that it is impossible to keep the right hand from knowing and being affected by what the left hand is doing. It may be difficult, but it is not impossible. Certainly it is inevitable that the satisfaction of purely meretricious standards for fiction will ultimately condition the writer to making the concessions before he is asked to do so by falling into the pattern offered by his market. Reduced to the simplest terms, an artist is a writer who writes only what he is impelled to write from within himself, whereas a professional writer will write whatever appears expeditious to him.

The writer may easily become a writing hack—that is, a writer who will write anything for cash, though it is far more likely that he will be given the label without having the profit presumed to go with it. The question of artistic integrity inevitably arises. If a writer who has patiently labored to create a character subsequently, at the behest of an editor, alters his manuscript to enable his character to do something which is fundamentally "out of character," that writer's artistic integrity may indeed be challenged. Such editorial requests are, of course, very seldom made. Moreover, the question of such creative integrity seldom arises for the

purely professional writer; the creative artist has the creation of as perfect a work as he can do as his goal, whereas
the professional writer's goal is the sale of his work. The artist demands ultimate publication as a necessary concession
to his ego, that is, his driving force, but the professional
writer looks upon publication only as another means of keeping his name before his public as much as possible, and,
apart from this, publication seldom means anything to him.
The professional writer is, in short, quite as much a businessman as the publisher.

But what happens to the writer who makes a determined
effort to create genuinely meritorious fiction on the one hand
and pure formula fiction for magazine publication on the
other? Thrusting aside the inevitable reaction of some critics
to the effect that his pulp affects his serious work (the reverse charge is seldom made, which is in itself very curious),
he will find that he must be constantly vigilant in order to
prevent just that from taking place. In most cases, the creative artist refuses to take seriously the professional writer;
I refer, obviously, to the two drives within one individual.
Just the same, however, if the creative artist has the integrity
every creative artist must have, he simply cannot permit
himself to write anything even in the professional field which
will not at least superficially pass muster before his creative
artist's eyes. If he has not, he may find it quite possible very
easily to yield to the greater facility of expression which
lies within the province of the professional writer, and is only
secondarily the privilege of the creative artist. For instance,
the professional writer need not devote as much time and
space to the presentation of any given character as the creative artist; this seeming facility may intrude upon the crea-

tive artist's drive. All this is more especially true in the writing of romantic fiction than of anything else, for the obvious reason that the field of romantic fiction is the broadest of all; it does not often occur in writing realistic fiction, which is by and large the work of creative artists as opposed to professional writers.

The creative artist may go to fantastic lengths to maintain his integrity. Most writers are familiar with the story of how the late Marcel Proust rose from his sick-bed to attend a ball for the sole purpose of ascertaining just how a certain French nobleman, a character in Proust's great novel, *Remembrance of Things Past,* wore his monocle. This was far from being an affectation, as the impressive integrity of Proust's novel gives ample evidence; this comparatively trivial detail was to Proust fully as important as any other aspect of his character's portrayal, and, as an artist, he could neither write nor rest until he had satisfied himself about it. I mention it here because it has often been quoted as an example of the artist's "temperament," and such it certainly is not; it has nothing to do with temperament, which is a psychological defense utilized by a) people who fancy themselves artists and manage to conceal their small talents behind outbursts of rudeness, bad manners, and grandiose egotism lest someone discover how trivial their talents really are; and b) genuine creative artists who deliberately affect it as a means of keeping off people who would otherwise take up time and who are so constituted that they could not understand and would take offense at a straightforward request to refrain from interruption, but who, at the same time, would dismiss simple bad manners or rudeness as what one might expect from an "artist", satisfying as it does a pre-conceived notion of what creative people are like.

The purely professional writer is concerned with artistic or creative integrity to a considerably less degree. It is not the creation of character, the exposition of a theme, or the weaving of an immortal story which is his problem; he is concerned simply with the telling of an interesting story. He may tell his story so well that his characters live more vividly than those of a genuinely better novel or short story. Paradoxically, he may set out to do a work of art and end up with a performance which is the envy of every professional writer. A case in point is Margaret Mitchell's *Gone With the Wind,* which is far from being a great novel or even an artistic work, but which is certainly entertaining, with characters who linger in memory long after the book has been read. Such an achievement is naturally the goal of every professional writer. *Gone With the Wind* is the last word in romanticism, a return to which in a major way was in progress even before the war, and continued during the war —the escape from bitter reality being a natural impulse for all of us. *Gone With the Wind* is professionally great, but it is not artistically so.

What does it matter? the novice may ask. It matters not at all. Greatness is in any case, artistically or professionally or by any other label, a relative matter. No writer sets out to write a "great" story in a deliberate pattern of writing technique. He sets out to write a good story that will sell, or one which will satisfy some drive or urge or compulsion within him, without regard for whether it will sell or not. If he sets out to write a "great" story, he is defeated almost before he starts. The fact is that factors beyond his control go into the making of a great story—historical timeliness, the mood and direction of the reading public, a public which has made phenomenal best-sellers of such a variety of books as *Anthony Adverse, Gone With the Wind, The Yearling, The Song of Bernadette, The Robe, For Whom the Bell Tolls,* and *A Bell for Adano*—books which are romantic, nostalgically young and regional, religiously romantic, and realistic with wartime realism and a touch of propaganda, which should serve again as an object lesson for the writer who would try his hand at something that might live—that the reading public is unpredictable in its tastes save in the very broadest sort of way which enables one to assume correctly that nothing will be so dead after the war as a book about war. Until enough time has passed to permit an Erich Maria Remarqué to come along again with such a bitterly realistic, disillusioning text as *All Quiet on the Western Front*—save that in World War II, no one needs any disillusion; it is manifest without the prompting of any work of fiction.

The writer of romantic fiction is in any case seldom impelled by such motives, which are far more likely to obsess the writer of realistic fiction. At best, the writer of romantic fiction may be motivated by the desire to do his best for a character or a theme. The love motivation of most romantic stories finds its most felicitous development in character and theme in a plot which on the whole remains fairly orthodox in that it can always be reduced to lover, beloved, and conflict—whether an old-fashioned, leering villain serves as conflict, or whether conflict is supplied by the weather, illness, schizophrenia, death, parents, rivalry, or any one of hundreds of other circumstances. The course of the story does not vary to any noteworthy degree; the movement is always toward the achievement of the same end—happiness with the beloved; the stage is set, the drive is made obvious, and conflict appears. Then for all the way from five to five hundred pages the conflict increases in intensity and it results inevitably, in a romantic story, in victory for the hero or heroine, from whosever point of view the story is told.

The search for variation in the fundamental conflict patterns of the romantic story has been given considerable help in new directions by the psychiatric revelations of the past few decades. In a melange of romantic stories within reach of me as I write, there is an instructive variety of conflict in the various love affairs therein chronicled—two feature the usual rivalry, one of them complicated by parental opposition; one features religious difference—a delicate subject; one, class difference; two, racial antagonism and intolerance; one, schizophrenia; one, the death of the hero's first wife and her haunting memory; and the final one, doubt. This last named seemed to me the most interesting in that its story was a simple, straightforward one of childhood sweethearts on the threshold of marriage, and I was curious to know how the author would introduce conflict, since no person or event seemed to loom on the horizon to promise it; he resolved the difficulty very adroitly by having the hero slowly fall prey to doubt about the wisdom of his direction, after which the novel fell into the conventional pattern of having the heroine's attentions to another suitor help the hero to make up his mind.

In the actual writing of the romantic story the novice should bear in mind in this order: his story, verisimilitude, movement, and dialogue. Story thus remains of paramount

interest, and its quality of conviction for the reader is sec
ond only to it; it should have reasonably well-paced move
ment, and its dialogue should sound natural. Successful dia
logue grows out of two things, primarily: observation of life
and author-identification with character. There is half a
century's difference between this proposal of 1890—

"My dearest Elaine, I dare to lay bare my heart. It would
give me the greatest happiness and make me feel very proud
if you would do me the honor to become my wife."

And this contemporary proposal—

"Look, baby—I got my raise, and it's good enough for
two to live on. What do you say?"

Generally, the same rules apply to dialogue whether it is
designed to be part of a realistic story, or of a romantic tale;
it must sound real; it must be the kind of dialogue the
reader might hear at any moment in the given circumstances.
Once the reader is annoyed by stilted language, or given
doubt by a lack of reality in dialogue, the writer has lost him.
The contemporary writer should have no difficulty about re
producing dialogue of his own time, but he is likely to en
counter trouble when he attempts to reproduce the dialogue
of a century ago, should he turn his hand to an historical
novel. In the majority of cases, he can resolve his difficulties
by keeping fairly close to natural, easy language, with the
addition of carefully chosen idioms of the time-period of the
novel.

Occasionally, special problems arise. In *Bright Journey*
I had to deal with two of them. One concerned the speech
of a well-known Wisconsin lady, whose memory was very
much alive among potential readers of the book. The lady
was of French origin, and spoke with an habitually strong

accent—so strong, indeed, that she actually wrote words in her letters very much as she pronounced them. Despite the fact that such accent is orthodox, it is often better avoided, but I felt that it could not be avoided in this case. I made a careful study of her speech patterns, and tried to reproduce it. The following is a sample of the dialogue as it appeared in the novel—

> "Have you arrange' for place to stay, Mistaire Dousman?" she asked.
> "No. No, I haven't. I could do that now, and perhaps when I come back Mr. Rolette might be here."
> "M'sieu' Rolette would expec' you to stay here, at leas' until you fin' place," she replied. "I am sairtain you will be comfortable here?" She said this with an almost imperceptible air of challenge. "Besides, M'sieu' Rolette is sairtain to come home."

Completely disregarding my intentions, most critics objected to what they termed her "stilted dialogue".

My second problem concerned the French *voyageurs* of the fur-trading country, and the Indians. Such Indian characters as those who could not speak any kind of English could be translated in summary very well, but those who did speak English offered the same kind of challenge as the *voyageurs*. I resolved to reproduce the language as accurately as possible from such records and sources as were available to me. The *voyageurs*, by and large, spoke like this:

> "I was for a while wit' Pierre Chouteau. I go wit' Manuel Lisa one trip. By gar! a man could not forgit dat trip. Dat was year of eart'quake: 1811. Dat was tam Astor's brigade he wen' up de Missouri, dat tam Hunt led."

But the Indians had not such a set pattern; their speech was not the result of a superimposing of one language upon another, allowing for a slow growth of dialect, as was the conversation of the French-Canadian or Canuck *voyageurs*. As I came upon one record after another, I discovered such an overwhelming variation in dialect that I was soon forced to abandon any attempt at its reproduction with any degree of exactness, and I fell back upon the traditional summary, even in conversation, so that instead of straight dialogue, whole pages were filled with one-sided dialogue or summaries, similar to the following:

> Thunder Walker reflected and presently made an elaborate count on his fingers. Actually only two of the chiefs knew of it; they were friendly chiefs; there was no danger in their knowledge. The white men in question, repeated Thunder Walker, had come from Fort Snelling and not from the meeting place of the rivers. There was no immediate danger, but if the tribe saw the soldiers going into the north, away from the fort, they would consider it a sign of weakness. Besides, there were the prisoners, Wamangoosgaraha and the other Winnebago who had killed the Methodes; they would certainly be taken along, if indeed they were not already dead; some of the Indians said so; it made them all want to take meat in the customary code of the Winnebagos, to kill two white people for every Indian slain; this was traditional; it could not be helped; it was the Winnebago law.

I "larded" such summaries whenever possible with direct translations of typical Indian phrases, to give them greater conviction. Thus—not the "confluence of the rivers" but "the meeting place of the rivers"; not "kill in revenge", but "take meat"; etc. The result was highly felicitous; much ground was covered in these conversations, and these summaries had a movement which the reproduction of the actual language would never, by any stretch of the imagination, have had.

If the writer intends to use dialect, he must take exceptional pains to keep it accurate and to refrain from using either too much or too difficult a dialect. If he also uses colloquialisms and other speech patterns, he should be sure of his ground, and he might also be aware of origins. Thus, a very common expression, "I could have died laughing!" has its prototype in local speech patterns in "I like t' a-died laughing," its genesis having been "I was likely to have died laughing." This has often become an expression of astonishment, "I like t' die," which is already a marked departure from its original use. The same thing is true of such a common expression as "I'll be dog-gonned," which can be heard as "I'll be dogged" or "I' be dog!" Writing of members of my own family from what I was certain was a predominantly Teutonic background, I was astonished to encounter common use of two exclamations which seemed to me of Anglican origin—"My conscience!" and "Heavens to Betsy!"—and traced them straight back through two German generations to an English strain I had not known was in the family.

As a general rule, dialect and most colloquialisms ought to be avoided in the romantic story; their place is properly in the realistic story, and their reproduction is not really necessary in the dialogue of the romantic story. Generally, too, extended characterizations may be left out of the romantic story; involved psychological explanations, excepting only insofar as they are necessary to the achievement of verisimilitude, ought likewise to be omitted.

There is one other aspect of writing the romantic story which the professional writer cannot ignore. That is familiarity with his market as well as with his material. If he makes a conscientious study of the way in which other writers have written, he will learn many little writing helps of all kinds. Each writer has his own methods, and something of those methods is usually always obvious in his work. Then, having done all this, the writer should study with equal care the magazines to which he intends to submit his stories. This may seem almost like unnecessary advice, but it is a well-known fact—particularly by editors—that all too many authors show no real knowledge of their markets. They can do without it if they employ an agent, but a majority of novices in writing cannot afford to employ an agent for their beginnings. Also, it should be made clear that by "study" I do not mean a simple reading of stories in any given magazine; no, a study should determine for the novice at writing just what there is about any chosen story which might make it acceptable to *Redbook* but never to *Cosmopolitan,* to *The American,* but never to *Collier's,* for instance. Unless he can learn to determine these factors, he is neglecting a necessary part of his education as a professional writer.

A Reading List

Love Stories

THE PIPER'S FEE, by Samuel Hopkins Adams (1925)
A LANTERN IN HER HAND, by Bess Streeter Aldrich (1928)
FIVE WOMEN, by Faith Baldwin (1942)
ARIZONA STAR, by Faith Baldwin (1945)
THE ROSARY, by Florence Barclay (1909)
EDNA HIS WIFE, by Margaret Ayer Barnes (1935)

VALIANT IS THE WORD FOR CARRIE, by Barry Benefield
  (1935)
YOUNG DR. KILDARE, by Max Brand (1941)
MAY FLAVIN, by Myron Brinig (1938)
NIGHT CLUB, by Katherine Brush (1929)
THE DELECTABLE MOUNTAINS, by Struthers Burt (1926)
WINDSWEPT, by Mary Ellen Chase (1941)
THE INSIDE OF THE CUP, by Winston Churchill (1913)
EAST OF BROADWAY, by Octavus Roy Cohen (1938)
THE YOUNG MRS. MEIGS, by Elizabeth Corbett (1931)
THELMA, by Marie Corelli (1887)
BAD GIRL, by Viña Delmar (1928)
AFTER NOON, by Susan Ertz (1926)
THE TRAIL OF THE LONESOME PINE, by John Fox, Jr.
  (1908)
THE BOOK OF CLAUDIA, by Rose Franken (1941)
BROOK EVANS, by Susan Glaspell (1928)
THREE WEEKS, by Elinor Glyn (1907)
GREEN DOLPHIN STREET, by Elizabeth Goudge (1944)
RAINBOW COTTAGE, by Grace Livingston Hill (1934)
THE CALIFORNIANS, by Louise Redfield Peattie (1940)
GOD'S COUNTRY AND THE WOMAN, by James Oliver Cur-
  wood (1915)
THE OLD HOME TOWN, by Rupert Hughes (1926)
EXPERIMENT, by Helen Hull (1940)
NIGHT OVER FITCH'S POND, by Cora Jarrett (1933)
THE VARMINT, by Owen Johnson (1910)
SCATTERGOOD BAINES, by Clarence Buddington Kelland
  (1921)
MIXED COMPANY, by Eleanor Mercein Kelly (1936)
MISS J. LOOKS ON, by Sophie Kerr (1935)

ALL THAT GLITTERS, by Francis Parkinson Keyes (1941)
CAPPY RICKS, by Peter B. Kyne (1916)
NOBODY'S GIRL, by Fanny Heaslip Lea (1940)
GALUSHA THE MAGNIFICENT, by Joseph C. Lincoln (1921)
ANNE OF GREEN GABLES, by L. M. Montgomery (1908)
THE FOUNTAIN, by Charles Morgan (1932)
BAKER'S DOZEN, by Kathleen Norris (1938)
BURNED FINGERS, by Kathleen Norris (1945)
A GIRL OF THE LIMBERLOST, by Gene Stratton Porter (1909)
THE HARVESTER, by Gene Stratton Porter (1911)
A KENTUCKY COLONEL, by Opie Read (1889)
MRS. WIGGS OF THE CABBAGE PATCH, by Alice Hegan Rice
    (1901)
TISH, by Mary Roberts Rinehart (1916)
LADIES GO MASKED, by Margaret Widdemer (1939)
REBECCA OF SUNNYBROOK FARM, by Kate Douglas Wiggin
    (1903)
RUGGLES OF RED GAP, by Harry Leon Wilson (1915)
THE RE-CREATION OF BRIAN KENT, by Harold Bell Wright
    (1919)

Western Stories

THE FORBIDDEN RIVER, by Harold Bindloss (1936)
CHIP OF THE FLYING U, by B. M. Bower (1904)
THE JACKSON TRAIL, by Max Brand (1932)
ACE IN THE HOLE, by Jackson Gregory (1941)
RIDERS OF THE PURPLE SAGE, by Zane Grey (1912)
HOPALONG CASSIDY, by Clarence E. Mulford (1910)
TANGLED TRAILS, by William MacLeod Raine (1921)
THE VIRGINIAN, by Owen Wister (1902)

Mystery and Detective Fiction

POLICE AT THE FUNERAL, by Margery Allingham (1932)

DEATH WALKS IN EASTREPPS, by Francis Beeding (1931)

THE KEEPER OF THE KEYS, by Earl Derr Biggers (1932)

THE SIMPLE WAY OF POISON, by Leslie Ford (1937)

FAREWELL, MY LOVELY, by Raymond Chandler (1940)

THE FIRST SAINT OMNIBUS, by Leslie Charteris (1939)

THE BISHOP MURDER CASE, by S. S. Van Dine (1929)

THE COMPLETE SHERLOCK HOLMES, by A. Conan Doyle (1930)

SPEAK NO EVIL, by Mignon Eberhart (1941)

THE THORNDYKE OMNIBUS, by R. Austin Freeman (1931)

THE CASE OF THE GOLDDIGGER'S PURSE, by Erle Stanley Gardner (1945)

THE HOUSE OF THE WHISPERING PINES, by Anna K. Green (1910)

THE THIN MAN, by Dashiell Hammett (1932)

THE BELLAMY TRIAL, by Frances Noyes Hart (1927)

THE EXPLOITS OF ARSENE LUPIN, by Maurice Leblanc (1907)

THE PHANTOM OF THE OPERA, by Gaston Leroux (1911)

THE LODGER, by Marie Belloc Lowndes (1913)

THE RASP, by Philip MacDonald (1924)

THE HOUSE OF THE ARROW, by A. E. W. Mason (1924)

SLIPPY MCGEE, by Marie Conway Oelmer (1917)

THE EVIL SHEPHERD, by E. Phillips Oppenheim (1923)

THE ADVENTURES OF JIMMY DALE, by Frank Lucius Packard (1917)

UNCLE ABNER, by Melville Davisson Post (1918)

CALAMITY TOWN, by Ellery Queen (1942)

THE CIRCULAR STAIRCASE, by Mary Roberts Rinehart (1908)

THE INSIDIOUS DR. FU MANCHU, by Sax Rohmer (1913)

THE NINE TAILORS, by Dorothy Sayers (1934)

MOSS ROSE, by Joseph Shearing (1934)

THE CRIME OF INSPECTOR MAIGRET, by Georges Simenon (1932)

THE CASE BOOK OF JIMMY LAVENDER, by Vincent Starrett (1944)

THE LEAGUE OF FRIGHTENED MEN, by Rex Stout (1935)

ALIAS THE LONE WOLF, by Louis Joseph Vance (1921)

WITHIN THE LAW, by Bayard Veiller (1917)

A KING BY NIGHT, by Edgar Wallace (1926)

THE MAN WITH THE CLUB FOOT, by Valentine Williams (1918)

Historical Romances

KING'S PASSPORT, by H. Bedford-Jones (1927)

THE HANDSOME ROAD, by Gwen Bristow (1938)

DYNASTY OF DEATH, by Taylor Caldwell (1938)

THE RAKE AND THE HUSSY, by Robert W. Chambers (1930)

ALL THIS, AND HEAVEN TOO, by Rachel Field (1938)

GRAUSTARK, by George Barr McCutcheon (1901)

WHEN KNIGHTHOOD WAS IN FLOWER, by Charles Major (1898)

GONE WITH THE WIND, by Margaret Mitchell (1936)

THE POWER AND THE GLORY, by Gilbert Parker (1925)

SCARAMOUCHE, by Rafael Sabatini (1921)

CAPTAIN FROM CASTILE, by Samuel Shellabarger (1945)

Adventure Fiction

GALLEGHER AND OTHER STORIES, by Richard Harding Davis
(1891)

MR. GLENCANNON, by Guy Gilpatric (1935)

THE CALL OF THE WILD, by Jack London (1903)

MUTINY ON THE BOUNTY, by Charles Nordhoff and James
Norman Hall (1932)

WHISPERING SMITH, by Frank H. Spearman (1906)

THE ADVENTURES OF EPHRAIM TUTT, by Arthur Train
(1930)

III: THE IMAGINATIVE STORY

The writing of imaginative fiction offers fewer strictures than does that of realistic or other romantic fiction—for, of course, imaginative fiction is in a sense a branch of romantic fiction. The writer may swing boldly off into the unknown; he does not need to bother with characterizations; he is at liberty to use stock figures, whether he is writing a tale of the supernatural or one of mystery-detection. Such a story as Donald Wandrei's *The Red Brain* is a notably successful example of the tale which has no ties to anything on earth.

However, the writer who is impelled toward imaginative fiction as his forte, will be advised to keep at least one foot solidly on familiar ground. Anything out of the ordinary is so much more effective in a familiar setting. Explaining his own credo, H. P. Lovecraft, author of the classic collection of supernatural tales, *The Outsider and Others* (1939), wrote in 1931: "To make a fictional marvel wear the momentary aspect of exciting fact, we must give it the most elaborate possible approach—building it up insidiously and gradually out of apparently realistic material, realistically handled. The time is past when adults can accept marvellous conditions for granted. Every energy must be bent toward the weaving of a frame of mind which shall make the story's single departure from nature seem credible—and in the weaving of this mood, the utmost subtlety and verisimilitude are required. In every detail *except* the chosen marvel, the story should be accurately true to nature. The keynote should be that of scientific exposition—since that is the normal way of presenting a 'fact' new to existing knowledge—and should not change as the story gradually slides off from the possible into the impossible. Spectral fiction should be realistic as well as atmospheric—confining its departure from nature to the one supernatural channel chosen, and remembering that scene, mood, and phenomena are more important in conveying what is to be conveyed than are characters and plot. The 'punch' of a truly weird tale is simply some violation or transcending of fixed cosmic law—an imaginative escape from palling reality—since phenomena rather than *persons,* are the logical 'heroes'. Horrors should be original—the use of common myths and legends being a weakening influence."

In the preface to his *Seven Famous Novels* three years later, H. G. Wells wrote: "In all this type of story the living interest lies in their nonfantastic elements and not in the invention itself. They are appeals for human sympathy quite as much as any 'sympathetic' novel, and the fantastic element, the strange property or the strange world, is used only to throw up and intensify our natural reactions of wonder, fear, and perplexity. . . . The thing that makes such imaginations interesting is their translation into commonplace terms and a rigid exclusion of other marvels from the story. Then it becomes human. . . . Nothing remains interesting where anything can happen."

These two quotations from writers in the genre of the imaginative ought to go a long way toward pointing the direction for the beginning writer. The fact is that, among the great body of fine imaginative literature available to present-day readers, comparatively little belongs to that particular school of thought which maintains that swinging boldly off into the unknown achieves the best result. In this regard, Donald Wandrei's *The Red Brain* is actually a superb achievement; it is an unearthly tale—not in the unearthly sense of Lord Dunsany's fantasies, nor of the strange timelessness of Olaf Stapledon's *Star Maker* or William Hope Hodgson's *The House on the Borderland*—but in a purely dissociated sense. *The Red Brain* is a "pure" interplanetary tale, a tale set in outer space, among distant universes, and it has no ties whatever to the mundane world we know, not even in that common tie so prevalent in tales of interplanetary travel—human beings. Yet it succeeds admirably. But its very success serves only to underscore the arguments of those who hold that the imaginative tale rising out of a familiar background carries the most drama for the average reader. The conclusion is overwhelming, after a study of the fiction in the field, that the sense of reality has first to be carefully instilled, and then with equal care to be insidiously undermined, so preparing the reader for the shock of discovery of the incredible.

The imaginative tale, as apart from romantic fiction as a whole, concerns itself primarily with the impossible, the incredible, the improbable, and includes various distinctly off-trail or out-of-pattern stories such as mystery fiction with overtones of the supernatural. Ghost stories, horror tales, science-fiction, and pure fantasy are the major types of the imaginative story, and all are represented by a considerable body of work, a surprising amount of which is on a far more literary plane than is the vast bulk of romantic fiction generally. The ghost story is inevitably supernatural; the horror story need not be. Science-fiction is not at all supernatural but is a kind of glorified adventure story in a fantastic setting. And fantasy embraces everything from dream-world concepts to whimsy.

The Horror Story

In the past two decades there has been evident an increasing development of a taste for horror and terror, both supernatural and material. It is not difficult to point to reasons for this; certainly the steady growth of the magazine, *Weird Tales,* and the comparative success of its imitators since 1923 is one of those reasons; just as surely, the war heightened a desire for escape fiction, and few tales offer as complete an escape from the mundane as the tale of supernatural horror.

This is a comparatively new development in American reading tastes. Curiously enough, the American reader has for a long time withstood the influence from abroad, where even the best-known writers inevitably turn at least once or twice to do a tale of supernatural terror. This is especially true of British writers; for the American literary roster can offer very few names to stand beside those of Thomas Hardy, Max Beerbohm, John Galsworthy, Charles Dickens, W. W. Jacobs, D. H. Lawrence, and many another, all of whom have written tales in the genre. Edith Wharton, true—but she stands almost alone among authors whose forte was not the weird tale; and even in this field, apart from the great writers of the last century, we have produced in this century only one writer worthy to stand with Arthur Machen, Algernon Blackwood, Walter de la Mare, E. F. Benson, M. R. James and their company—H. P. Lovecraft.

It is a little too easy to fall back upon the excuse that

there has been no market for good tales of terror and horror, for that is simply not true. Manifestly, the obvious market has been *Weird Tales*, and for a short time there were also such fine markets as *Strange Tales, Unknown Worlds,* and *Strange Stories;* but these were short-lived. But the really good tale of terror or horror, supernatural or otherwise, is always assured a reception at editorial desks varying widely, all the way from *Charm* to *Collier's*, from *Harper's* to the *Atlantic*. True, there is not a great amount of space available in such magazines for off-trail stories—for the tale of horror is still an off-trail story to American editors in general—but there is room, quite apart from *Weird Tales,* which has itself a distinguished history, having published in its pages not only the bulk of the work of the late great H. P. Lovecraft and Henry S. Whitehead, but also such American masters of the macabre tale as Clark Ashton Smith, Frank Belknap Long, Robert Bloch, Donald Wandrei, and others, among the English writers of the genre—Machen, Blackwood, Benson.

The tale of horror falls easily enough into several classifications, but all types can ultimately be grouped under two heads—that of supernatural horror, and that of psychological (or material) horror. The tale of pure grue properly belongs under the latter head, but it may be regarded as in a separate classification, for few readers today any longer like the tale of pure physical horror. The gruesome story has descended virtually unchanged from the old Gothic novel, save only in style of writing, and its effectiveness is usually questionable. There has been little development in the tale of cold grue, apart from the French *conte cruel* (of which Maurice Level and Villiers de L'isle Adam are the best-known exponents), since the days of the original rattling skeletons and werewolves. In the early days of *Weird Tales*, tales of ghouls usually aroused a storm of protest and revulsion; but today's ghoul tale stirs scarcely a ripple.

The tale of psychological horror—that development indicated by Dorothy Sayers, when she wrote in a preface some years ago that we have progressed from the evil outside of us to that inside—is best exemplified by the work of Saki, Thomas Burke, and John Collier, whose much-reprinted *Thus I Refute Beelzy* is a minor classic of its kind. *Thus I Refute Beelzy* is a tale which some critics have interpreted as indicative of the evil in childhood, or the potential evil of children. It is an unmotivated tale of Small Simon, who, having no one else to play with, attracts an invisible playmate whom he calls Beelzy—(the cognoscenti will recognize the diminutive of Beelzebub)—and who finally turns upon Big Simon, a nagging sort of parent, who has it coming, and literally tears him apart. The classic last line tells the whole story of what happened upstairs in Small Simon's room to which Big Simon had repaired to punish his son for "lying" about Beelzy. Mrs. Carter, the lad's mother, had gone toward the stairs. "It was on the second-floor landing that they found the shoe, with the man's foot still in it, like that last morsel of a mouse which sometimes falls from the jaws of a hasty cat." For more of the same, see *Presenting Moonshine*, or *A Touch of Nutmeg and More Unlikely Stories*.

Such great tales of supernatural horror as Henry James's *The Turn of the Screw*, Arthur Machen's *The White People, The Novel of the White Powder, The Novel of the Black Seal*, E. F. Benson's *Negotium Perambulans*,

M. R. James's *Casting the Runes* and *Count Magnus*,
Algernon Blackwood's *The Willows*, Oliver Onions's *The
Beckoning Fair One*, Edith Wharton's *Afterward* are
easily available in current anthologies; so are such outstand-
ing stories of psychological horror as R. L. Stevenson's
Markheim, Conrad Aiken's *Mr. Arcularis* and *Silent Snow,
Secret Snow*, Walter de la Mare's *Seaton's Aunt*, and Char-
lotte Perkins Gilman's *The Yellow Wall Paper*.

Very often the combination of supernatural and physical
horror is eminently successful, and, of such combinations,
probably no more memorable story has been written by an
American since 1900 than H. P. Lovecraft's *The Rats in
the Walls*, which is currently in print in both *Sleep No More*
and *Great Tales of Terror and the Supernatural*.

The Rats in the Walls is the story of Mr. Delapore, an
American, who, having lost his son in World War I, returns
to his ancestral home in England, an abandoned ruin known
as Exham Priory, and prepares to restore it. The story is told
in retrospect, in an evident frantic desire to see what has
happened clearly and without illusion. For that reason, the
narrative, written in first person, proceeds leisurely and with
an apparent if strained attempt to be logical at all times.
The narrator, therefore, chronicles with obvious reluctance
the strange and frightening hints about "what went on" at
Exham Priory not just a decade ago, but centuries ago; he
admits that something scampering in the newly built walls
of the ruin, like the sound of thousands of rats, sent his cat,
Nigger-Man, into a frenzy; he finally concedes that there
must have been something terrible happening at this place,
for there is a cold, residual horror about the building, which
infests him as dampness infests old stone walls. Spurred on

by tales of curious and horrible "rites" supposed to have involved human sacrifice, Delapore and his neighbor, the plump Captain Norrys, determine to investigate. And, in so doing, they discover not only a subcellar, but a charnel ramification of underground passages leading to a bone-strewn place, apparently of Devil-Worship, so that it is evident that the ancestral Delapores were engaged in the most shocking and revolting rites, in traffic with beings out of the earth and out of hell. There is yet more to be discovered, and this comes cataclysmically to the reader when, after a burst of impassioned writing which betrays the state of the narrator's mind, he concludes with one terrible paragraph:

> That is what they say I said when they found me in the blackness after three hours; found me crouching in the blackness over the plump, half-eaten body of Captain Norrys, with my own cat leaping and tearing at my throat. Now they have blown up Exham Priory, taken my Nigger-Man away from me, and shut me into this barred room at Hanwell with fearful whispers about my heredity and experiences. Thornton is in the next room, but they prevent me from talking to him. They are trying, too, to suppress most of the facts concerning the priory. When I speak of poor Norrys they accuse me of a hideous thing, but they must know that I did not do it. They must know it was the rats; the slithering scurrying rats whose scampering will never let me sleep; the daemon rats that race behind the padding in this room and beckon me down to greater horrors than I have ever known; the rats they can never hear; the rats, the rats in the walls.

No résumé of this fine story can do it justice, and the potential writer of horror tales should most emphatically read it to appreciate Mr. Lovecraft's carefully restrained build-up for that unutterably horrible climax.

The writer who contemplates writing a tale of horror should bear in mind that the same general rules apply to writing horror fiction that apply to the writing of any other kind of fiction. But it is important especially in horror fiction to avoid extraneous material; any digression ought not only to lead back to the central horror theme, but ought to contribute something to it. If the story is one of supernatural horror, by all means avoid any suggestion of a natural explanation; there is nothing even remotely like a natural explanation for spoiling what might otherwise have been a good tale of supernatural horror.

H. P. Lovecraft succeeded primarily because he managed to make convincing the most outré horrors simply by the expedient of utilizing not only the known world but also some of its most prosaic aspects to convey horror—note especially his use of the phonograph in the novelette, *The Whisperer in Darkness*. Lovecraft believed also that a horror not quite seen was considerably more effective than a horror fully seen. This allows full play on the part of the reader's imagination; if, however, the reader is devoid of imagination, as many people are, he belongs to the group who will write to the editor to complain that the author's horror was "too vague". The writer, of course, must make the compromise; and he must compromise not with his readers, but with himself. If he is at his best with a horror not quite fully visualized, then by all means let him utilize it and make no effort to bring his horror into sharp focus. The technique of revealing a little at a time, as in *The Rats*

the Walls, climaxing in a final detail which explains the
whole horror in retrospect, is especially to be recommended.

The experienced writer in the genre will avoid too much
true; he will shy away from a heavy ladling on of horror,
preferring a subtler approach; and therefore the beginner
is well-advised to follow his example. The writer ought also
himself to believe in his horror at least for the duration of
his writing; believe it or not, disbelief on the part of the
writer is intangibly reflected in the story. It is quite possible
to pick up a copy of *Weird Tales* and pick out those stories
written with "belief" and those written purely for commer-
cial ends. Moreover, a careful choice of words and phrases
can do much to lend uncanniness to the tale of terror and
the supernatural, making plain the cleavage between the
horror tale, which most often has a supernatural or psychiatric explanation, and the mystery-terror tale, which has a
perfectly scientific explanation.

Of all the don'ts for horror fiction writers, however, there
is one which stands out pre-eminently. And that is: don't
try to write a comic horror tale. There have been repeated
printings of stories purporting to be of horror or supernatural terror which are written not only as comedy, but with
almost ribald flippancy. Such stories are most emphatically
not horror stories; they are outright comedy, and their presentation as ghost tales, terror tales, or the like is a simple
fraud. Comedy and horror simply do not mix; they are anti-
pathetic. Even worse is flippancy. One does not think of
Thorne Smith's *Topper* as a ghost story at all, but as a
comic novel; Smith himself never made any other claim for
it. The same is true of Oscar Wilde's much-reprinted and

delightful tale, *The Canterville Ghost,* which is first and foremost a comic satire on Americans in England, and only by courtesy of having a ghost in it a ghost tale. It is frankly impossible for a comic tale to be horrible, and, regardless of vociferous proponents of the comic gruesome tale, the cognoscenti disdain them. It should be pointed out, however, that quite the contrary is true of the tale of fantasy, which, as Eric Knight and many others have demonstrated, can be delightfully funny and at the same time fantastic—though there are no elements of terror or horror.

Curiously enough, horror in fiction is an escape from horror in real life. It is paradoxical that this is so, but the demand for collections of horror stories among the Editions for Armed Services during World War II bears testimony to the fact. By what rationale men and women who have had experiences which must be among the most horrible experiences of which man is capable should turn to horror fiction in order to get away from real life, one is hard put to it to say. But it is not necessary to seek an explanation; the fact exists, and the alert writer will satisfy the demand for horror fiction if he is capable of writing it. His capability depends upon his ability to give credibility to his theme, to believe in his own horror, and to present it in such a way that it will linger nastily to haunt his reader's memory for at least a few hours after it has been read—the way the rats in the walls of Lovecraft's story do, for instance, or the strange beings surrounding the house on the borderland in Hodgson's novel of that name, or the way in which the little people lurk on the borders of consciousness in Arthur Machen's superb tales.

he Ghost Story

In the frankly supernatural tale, a strong realistic back-
:ound is even more necessary than in the tale of horror.
[orror, after all, is a part of human experience in its biologi-
ıl and mental aspects, ·if not in the supernatural facets. A
host is by its very nature something alien to this world; hor-
)r is not. The traditional concept of a ghost as a spectral
nage of one dead is no longer inclusive enough, however,
)r a contemporary definition. In the foreword to *Who*
nocks? I wrote that a ghost story was "any tale in which the
nimating force is in the nature of a return from the dead.
'hat includes not only the old-fashioned spectre, transparent
nd easily recognized as a representation of someone dead,
ut also everything else from psychic residue to lycanthropic
ıanifestations." This definition may quite possibly fall short
f satisfying every devotee of the genre, but it seems to me
ıclusive enough to allow for every variation.

The masters of the ghost story—that is, the absolute,
ormative masters after the Gothic period in English litera-
ıre—have seemed to me to be a mere handful in number—
. Sheridan Le Fanu, Dr. Montague Rhodes James, Mary E.
Vilkins-Freeman, and Algernon Blackwood; after them
ome E. F. Benson, May Sinclair, H. R. Wakefield, Edith
Vharton, Walter de la Mare, and certain others who have
ritten less prolifically in the field. Le Fanu represents the
est in the old-fashioned tale of the supernatural; he was
riting when the Gothic tale was still enjoying a sort of
ogue, but his stories—particularly the novels, *Uncle Silas*
nd *The House by the Churchyard,* and the short story col-
:ction, *In a Glass Darkly*—are realistically presented in a

prose style far superior to that employed by most of tl
Gothic novelists. Dr. James, and more recently, Dean R.]
Malden (*Nine Ghosts*), have acknowledged the influence
Le Fanu. James's work is quite clearly in the orthodox trac
tion of Le Fanu, but he manages to reach heights nev
before or since surpassed in his creation of memorably te
rible spectres, while Algernon Blackwood tends to emphasi
the mystical, almost pantheistically, which such class
stories as *The Willows, Running Wolf, The Wendigo*, ar
The Listener illustrate very well.

Dr. Montague Rhodes James in England, and Mary .
Wilkins-Freeman in America were particularly notewortl
in that they took exceptional care to prepare an unmista
ably recognizable setting. In the ghost stories of Dr. Jame
there is an inevitability about the spectre in every case, :
inevitability which is inescapable. He preferred settings wi
which he himself was comprehensively familiar; his inte
ests were archaeological and architectural; he was Provo
at Eton, and had written many ecclesiastical and antiquaria
works prior to his work in the field of the supernatural. It
therefore not surprising that his ghost story settings are ve
often cathedrals, ruined abbeys, and so forth; he typifi
the writer who gains an especially forceful effect by virt
of keeping close to familiar ground in his settings.

Mrs. Freeman did likewise. In her non-weird short storie
the regional New England background is presented wi
great fidelity. She wrote but a single book of ghost storie
but other spectral tales are scattered among volumes
other short stories. Her style is spare, her details excellent
chosen, her writing manner easy and flexible. Her best sto
is perhaps *The Shadows on the Wall*, an examination

which discloses that it seems to be a story of crime, rather than a ghost story. It is disarmingly told, and there is practically no movement as the writer of an action story would understand it. The majority of the story emerges almost elliptically, in fragmentary conversation.

Briefly, *The Shadows on the Wall* concerns the poisoning of Edward Glynn by his parsimonious and bad-tempered brother, Dr. Henry Glynn. When the story opens, the surviving sisters—Miss Rebecca, Miss Caroline, and Mrs. Emma Brigham are discussing Edward's sudden death. Edward and Henry, it appeared, had had words in the study the night before Edward died. Henry had not made any threats about Edward's easygoing way, but—

> "But what?"
> "I saw him when he came out of this room."
> "He looked mad?"
> "You've seen him when he looked so."

And then,

> "Do you remember that time he killed the cat because she had scratched him?"

From this, and a very little that has gone before, the reader gets a surprisingly clear picture of Henry, so that when he is actually introduced into the story, the few lines of succinct physical description Mrs. Freeman gives him are almost superfluous. Tension is there, and it mounts. There is no hint of anything spectral in cerements. There is no suggestion of anything more than something a little strange about Edward's death—he had had words with the bad-tempered Henry, who had signed his death certificate; Henry

had once killed that cat in fury; Henry may not have liked
his easygoing brother, Edward, but the sisters did; there
was that curious reluctance on the part of any one of the
three of them to put into words what was going on behind
their eyes. The reader is, in fact, so concerned with the ques
tion of whether or not Henry killed Edward, that the ghost
when it does come, has been on the scene for quite a while be
fore the reader becomes fully aware of it.

That may seem paradoxical, but it is not so; it is in the
nature of a tribute to Mrs. Freeman. The ghost is not an
apparition in the usual sense at all; it makes its appearance
very unobtrusively, though, in retrospect, the reader will
begin to understand that some of the apprehension of the
two sisters who lived in the house concerned itself with what
they had seen in the study previous to the time of the opening scene. The ghost, then, is simply a shadow on the wall;
it is not even a clear shadow in the lamplight, but there is
enough of it to suggest Edward Glynn. The shadow does
nothing; it makes no gestures; it does not turn; it is simply
there. The sisters have already moved everything in the
room, thinking it is a trick shadow brought on by some arrangement of the furniture with the lamp, and subsequently,
Henry comes in and tries in every way to determine what
object or arrangement of objects is casting this unusual
shadow. It is almost ridiculously prosaic, and particularly so
in so bald a summary as this; but it is actually anything but
prosaic. No one wants to say what he thinks; no one men-
tions a ghost; the most that passes among the sisters is the
admission that it looks like Edward, but "It *must* be something in the room." Finally it comes out that this ominous

shadow has been on the wall since the night of the day of
Edward's unexpected death.

Henry's rage eventually comes to the surface. He, too,
rearranges everything; he carries on briefly like a wild man,
but then he laughs and straightens everything up. "A man is
a fool to try to account for shadows," he says. Nevertheless,
he tries repeatedly to account for it, and, failing to do so, he
leaves immediately after the funeral to go to the city for
three days. When he does not arrive on the last train at the
end of the three days, Mrs. Brigham is impelled to go to the
study to see whether the shadow is still there. Caroline follows her, while Rebecca goes to answer the doorbell.

> Caroline and her sister Emma entered the study.
> Caroline set the lamp on the table. They looked at the
> wall. "Oh, my God," gasped Mrs. Brigham, "there are
> —there are *two* shadows." The sisters stood clutching
> each other, staring at the awful things on the wall. Then
> Rebecca came in, staggering, with a telegram in her
> hand. "Here is—a telegram," she gasped. "Henry is—
> dead."

That is all. There is nothing to tell you without evasion
that Dr. Henry Glynn killed himself in the city, afraid to
come back and face that awful shadow on the wall. It does
not seem like much of a story, but nevertheless it is a reading experience, and you will remember those terrifying
shadows on the wall for a long time.

A shadow on the wall for a ghost is even today rather
novel, though it is more than three decades old. But contemporary ghosts manifest themselves in all manner of
guises; the day of the headless horseman who pursued poor

old Ichabod Crane has long since gone by, though the skill
ful presentation of another such today would not be shunned
by the devotees of the weird. The ghost of today, however
manifests itself in an astonishing variety of ways; it may be
in a rush of air, a disembodied voice, a light, a sound (as
distinct from the traditional Gothic clanking of chains and
hollow groans); it may come into being by means of a
photograph, a chant, a crime, an accident; and, even when
the dread spectre is itself visible, it may have any one of a
number of appearances quite apart from the expected ap
pearance of one dead. Dr. James's ghosts are, on the whole
a nauseatingly hideous company, certainly not the kind of
company you would want to meet in your dreams, much less
in waking hours. Mrs. Freeman's, on the other hand, are not
hideous at all; they are often almost moral ghosts; yet they
are potent, mysterious, and chilling—a triumph for her quiet
unadorned prose style.

The influence of Mrs. Freeman's quietly excellent ghost
stories has never been very wide; in her own time a handful
of now no longer known ladies followed her lead and wrote
ghost stories, some of which were collected by W. D. Howells
for his *Shapes That Haunt the Dusk.* But at least two writers
improved upon her pattern in the genre, and they were Edith
Wharton, whose omnibus collection, *Ghosts,* contains her best
work in the field, and the novelist, R. E. Spencer, whose *The
Lady Who Came to Stay* is one of the finest full-length ghost
stories ever published in America. To a certain extent I,
myself, have imitated her pattern, particularly in what is
perhaps my best story in the genre, *The Panelled Room,*
still in print in the Phil Stong anthology, *25 Modern Tales of
Mystery and Imagination.*

The ghost story, of course, is one of the oldest kinds of tales known. The lore of ghosts goes back into the folk history of every people and race. It is only natural that this should be so, because the ghost story's effectiveness lies in man's fear of the unknown as well as in his curiosity about death and what may come after. The motivations of the Gothic spectre were often only as stage effect or as the lesser villain of the piece; subsequently the ghost came to have a moral right to existence, appearing to avenge a crime or to jog a lax conscience, and so forth.

The novice in the field of the ghost story ought to make sure that his ghost is well-motivated. Granting the novice a well-constructed setting, his next task is adequacy of motivation. Now, that does not mean that a ghost, in order to appear, must have a reason of its own, such as vengeance, for instance. Nothing of the sort. By "motivation" in a ghost story, the reference may be to an adequate excuse for being apart from *motive* as motive alone. A ghost which appears to direct vengeance against his killer has a motive, clearly; a ghost which appears and terrorizes innocent people can be infinitely more horrible. When a ghost serves as an avenger, the reader's reaction is very often one of justifiable relish. "The wretch had it coming," he tells himself. Manifestly, this is not a particularly shocked reaction. It is quite the contrary when innocent people are caught up in a web of supernatural horror; in reading such a story the reader is far more likely to be frightened. "This might happen to me," he tells himself, with that delightful egotism which is so much a part of all of us, since in telling himself so he announces that he considers himself as innocent as the victims of the monster of the printed page.

The ghost, then, which has no such obvious motive as vengeance, but appears simply as a manifestation of incarnate evil, is apt to be far more effective insofar as readers are concerned. The avenging ghost, however terrible he may be, is after all a moral ghost; it is poetic justice which is the aim of the writer in such a ghost story. But in the story of the ghost for the sake of evil alone, there is no moral on the horizon. That is not to say that a moral ghost story cannot be terrible. One of the most frightening ghost stories in English is also one of the most moral. W. W. Jacobs's *The Monkey's Paw* is as moral as a Bible lesson. Moreover, it is a notable classic for another reason: its ghost offers weighty evidence in behalf of those who contend that a ghost unseen or half seen is infinitely more terrible than one which emerges in the clear moonlight, so to speak, for the ghost remains offstage in one of the most hair-raising climaxes in the genre. Another moral ghost story which is fully as successful, though for another reason, is Stevenson's *Markheim*.

But in the long run, which is to say, in the average, the moral ghost story must take second place. Compared to such tales of incarnate evil as Henry James's *The Turn of the Screw* and the stories of Arthur Machen, the average moral ghost tale is a pale thin performance indeed. All the manifestations in the tales of H. P. Lovecraft are evil for the sake of being evil and leave a shocking trail of madness and death, all of which is pleasantly horrible for the reader of weird tales, who is seemingly immune from really major shock and has an insatiable appetite for grue, ghosts, and things that go bump in the night.

Dr. Montague Rhodes James maintained that a ghost

ought properly to be "malevolent and odious." H. P. Love-craft held that any manifestation of the strange and extra-terrestrial was inherently terrible simply because it violated the known laws of space, time, or other fundamental con-cepts. In the prefatory pages to his fine anthology, *The Haunted Omnibus,* Alexander Laing expresses the belief that a "good ghost story should concern itself with matters worthy of our interest and attention." That is giving the writer every latitude, and in general seems a far more satisfying condition than those proposed by many writers of the genre. It includes, also, the necessary setting of the stage.

Perhaps far more than any other kind of story, the spectral tale must have an adequate and convincing stage setting, and the more commonplace the props, the better. Because of the Gothic novel, one expects an ancient castle to have its ghost; but a modern drawing-room is the last place in the world one might expect to find one. I have myself a fondness for gentry who scoff at the supernatural and are suddenly put face to face with it. Like Mr. Alexander Bramwell of *Bram-well's Guardian.* The story is typical of a method, and may be helpfully examined for the benefit of the novice.

Mr. Bramwell "was a methodical, unimaginative man . . . a confirmed putterer . . . the kind of elderly gentleman who cannot resist the temptation to poke his cane down a hole to see whether or not some creature will show itself." The crux of the description is, of course, in Mr. Bramwell's methodical unimaginativeness. You see at once that he is, so to speak, asking for it, and you know that very soon he is going to have a very unpleasant surprise because he is going to poke his stick down the wrong hole. He does. He unearths a curious ring in a little cairn on Salisbury Plain, and thereafter he is astonished beyond measure to find that people ask him whether "the other gentleman" is with him, and so on. Bramwell sees no other gentleman, but virtually everyone else does. He is angry with his man, and his acquaintances; lacking imagination, he naturally assumes they are having him. But Bramwell recalls that he did see a curious gentleman who had appeared on the Plain shortly after his taking of the buried ring, and so he goes to see his old friend, Skelton, who tells him that his ring is Druidic in origin, and that it has a guardian. "Put that ring back where you got it and cover it up again." The ring's guardian, insists Skelton, would destroy anyone who did not replace the ring in good time. Bramwell, of course, knows better. "You people have queer beliefs," he says shortly. Bramwell "had always scorned the imaginative life, and made no secret of it," and his friend Skelton's story was "folderol" and "the implausible creation of superstitious primitives." Ultimately, however, Bramwell does see his guardian in the night, and, while he believes nothing, he resolves to get rid of the ring by sending it to Skelton, who had professed some fear of it.

He does so, and he has hardly got rid of it when something happens to him, "something that might have come from the *Arabian Nights* . . . a monstrous dark thing, like billowing smoke, with vengeful green eyes" bears down on him out of a corner of the room . . .

> Botkins found him, and was a pitiable object for the few years remaining to his life. Indeed, Bramwell was scarcely recognizable; he was in at least four pieces, and had obviously undergone something frightful. "Blown up by an unknown explosive," said the coroner weightily.

As for Skelton: he was wise and imaginative. He took the first train to Salisbury Plain, with the ring in his pocket.

I do not venture to say just how far the sardonic and ironic may be carried along in a ghost story. Just as comedy is by and large suspect, irony may come under the interdict. It depends very largely on the writer's ability to tell a story well enough to diminish the irony sufficiently so that it does not intrude upon the reader's consciousness until he is ready for its brief impact. The stage setting may leave room for it at the right moment, accepting the fact that such stage setting may concern itself with a character or characters without reference to an actual place. Mr. Bramwell, for instance, can be found the world over; he happened to live in London, but the reader will recognize him instantly. He is that same fellow who picks up a copy of *Weird Tales* and asks in a patronizing voice, "Why on earth do you read this tripe?" You feel momentarily sorry for Mr. Bramwell, but, after all, he *was* told, he had his warnings in more ways than one, and if he insisted on being so obtuse, well . . . And there, of course, you have the key to the particular technique.

The reader is not particularly frightened by the ghost at all. The writer has made no attempt to frighten the reader. He has simply let him in on a secret, stirred up a kind of irritation at the leading character because of his lack of imagination, and carried him along to let him in on what is going to happen to Mr. Bramwell. This is as much a legitimate ghost story as the tale of spectral vengeance or the tale of cosmic evil of which H. P. Lovecraft was master. The reader knows all along that something is bound to happen to Mr. Bramwell and that he will have brought it on himself.

Well and good, he will think. It serves him right. The alliance between this sort of sardonic or ironic tale and the frankly moral ghost story is thus clearly established in reader-reaction.

But the tale of the evil apparition appearing without such commonplace motivation arouses an entirely different set of reactions. It causes a man to look uneasily over his shoulder, as E. F. Benson puts it, or to feel that if he is not careful, something of this sort may happen to him, as Dr. James writes. All these tales gain their effect primarily by the skill of the writer into cajoling his reader to experience these reactions, and he can best achieve this by keeping as much as possible to common human experience in characters and settings. The writer should accept at once that the only difference between a good short story and a good ghost story is that the latter has a ghost in it. He has admittedly a slightly more difficult task in making his ghost story convincing. After all, it is easy enough to write a ghost story for the devotee of the form, because he not only expects an apparition, but demands one. It is a different thing altogether to convince a non-believer even sometimes against his determination that for this brief time of the reading of your story there is such a thing as a ghost.

And the ghost story ought to be written as if every potential reader were an avowed skeptic. You don't challenge the shadows on the wall in Mrs. Freeman's fine story any more than you doubt the forces which brought about the horrible conclusion of Lovecraft's horror tale, *The Rats in the Walls*. You accept them, because the author's skill impels you to do so, even though you may tell yourself that of course, *scientifically* speaking, the concepts are quite impossible. But the imaginative tale is the antithesis of the scientific premise, and no reader is likely to approach a ghost story with the gleam of science in his eye. No reader, that is, but one—and that is the devotee of the tale of pseudo-science, who stands ever ready to shout hosannahs to announce the advance discovery of some new scientific principle or invention by one of the intrepid writers who expend their creative energy in imaginative science.

The Science-Fiction Story

Fundamentally, seven out of every ten science-fiction stories are only orthodox adventure tales with the trappings of interplanetary travel. The difference lies primarily in this: that instead of a traditional villain who also wants the girl, a host of Martians, Venusians, or what have you, serve as villains in the piece against a background of extensions of known scientific concepts into the realm of the extremely fanciful. Edgar Rice Burroughs' Martian tales are prototypes, and the basic theme seldom varies—motivated by a variety of events such as a terrestrial plague, a vital interest in rocket-ships, the noble impulse to be sacrificed to science, and so forth, the hero and the heroine, who is sometimes a stowaway, set forth bravely into the interstellar spaces. They duly arrive at the moon, Mars, Venus, or some hitherto unknown world or galaxy, and there immediately encounter creatures who are inimical to them (probably because of previous knowledge of man's history relative to wars, racial and religious intolerance, etc.), and there begins a titanic struggle for the girl, who, strangely, seems also to be an object of especial interest to the insectivorous or batrachian or reptilian inhabitants of this extra-terrestrial place. After a series of harrowing adventures, which may or may not include a full-scale war between worlds, the hero fetches the heroine back from hideous captivity, and they make the rocket-ship or the interstellar patrol just in time, with a horde of ravening citizens of this alien world at their heels.

That is the sum and substance of a majority of pseudo-science stories. Anyone with any writing ability at all, and enough fundamental knowledge of science to enable him to use the jargon with some imagination, ought to be able to write this kind of science-fiction. Its characters are stock, whether called Jack or Bo-Hok or X-5972; its plot is the plot of the most orthodox romance fiction—aspiration (object: matrimony), conflict, achievement, and, in time, even its extra-terrestrial background becomes as familiar as the usual background of the romantic tale. This particular type of imaginative fiction exists in relation to the field as a whole on the same plane as that occupied by the confession story in relation to the genre of romantic fiction.

There is, however, quite another type of science-fiction, and it is this type which commands the respect of every literate reader. It might be described simply as every kind of science-fiction which does not fall into the classification of the usual. Among its most representative titles are Olaf Stapledon's *Star Maker* and *Last and First Men*, H. G. Wells's *The Time Machine* and *The War Between the Worlds*, H. P. Lovecraft's *At the Mountains of Madness*, T. S. Stribling's *The Green Splotches*, C. S. Lewis's *Out of the Silent Planet*, H. F. Heard's *The Great Fog* and *Wingless Victory*, Robert Heinlein's *They*, Stephen Vincent Benét's *By the Waters of Babylon*, A. E. Van Vogt's *The World of $\bar{A}$*, and others.

The vogue for science-fiction began, insofar as the contemporary taste is concerned, with Mary Shelley's *Frankenstein* and with Jules Verne, whose *Twenty Thousand Leagues Under the Sea, From the Earth to the Moon,* and a score of others paved the way for the work of H. G. Wells and the later fiction of Stapledon, Lewis, *et al.* The primary motivation of the science-fiction tale is speculation about the progress of science and invention, and the devotees of the form are currently having a good time pointing out not only that Jules Verne foretold a great many things which came true after his death but that science-fiction writers in the early days of the post World War I revival of interest in the genre (which began with the establishment of *Amazing Stories* in 1925), have seen some of their wildly improbable inventions become fact—particularly those stories which were concerned with television, rockets and rocket travel, and atomic power.

Manifestly, of course, the accurate foretelling of coming scientific inventions is not the goal of the science-fiction writer or reader. Both are concerned with a good story utilizing some phase of science. Some readers like their stories heavily laden with the jargon of science, some prefer just enough to lend a story a feeling of authenticity. No matter what it is he writes in the field, the novice should know his science well enough so that he will not be apt to blunder, for readers are quick to correct errors in hypotheses, etc., made by the science-fiction writer, as any examination of the *Brass Tacks* column of *Astounding Science-Fiction* magazine will prove.

Next to death and what is beyond death, nothing so fascinates mankind as the mystery of the cosmos, of outer space. The concept of the universes beyond our own, of galaxies and distant suns, so remote that if man were able to travel with the speed of light, it would take more than a lifetime to reach them—this is a concept so vast, so alien to terrestrial existence, so fraught with wonder and terror and possibilities which challenge the imagination, that the sensitive mind is inevitably drawn to contemplation of it. And, even though there is no answer to the thousands of questions which come to mind, science-fiction nevertheless offers speculation, even if but of the most superficial sort, and at the same time entertains.

Hand in hand with the mysteries of outer space go the mysteries of the lacunae in the structure of terrestrial science. There are such lacunae. We have documentary evidence of phenomena which scientific men have simply denied because to have admitted such phenomena would have meant a complete re-examination of hitherto accepted scientific rules. A great deal of it has been gathered into four books by the late Charles Fort, now collected into an omnibus entitled *The Books of Charles Fort* (1941). Fort, a vociferous enemy of the dogmatic, challenged scientific credos with accounts of the strange events which so far science has not explained.

Such inexplicable events naturally stir the imagination; in them lie the bases for countless science-fiction stories, for the imaginative tale of pseudo-science is by no means limited to interplanetary travel. It may range from a purely mathematical hypothesis like that in Harry Stephen Keeler's *John Jones' Dollar* to a tale of time travel like H. P. Lovecraft's *The Shadow Out of Time;* it may concern a fantastic concept of the end of the race as in Harry Bates's *Alas, All Thinking!* or a strange, intellectual race of penguins as in H. F. Heard's *Wingless Victory*. There is actually no limit to its subjects, provided they stem from science and are imaginative in concept, rather than realistic. Clearly, however, a story about a man's difficulties with his car or television set does not classify as pseudo-science, because these things are now part and parcel of our daily existence and are no longer in the realm of the imaginative.

After the interplanetary tale, there are a great number of gambits open to the novice in the field. He may have his choice among imagined inventions, strange, unexplored corners of the earth, sudden inexplicable reversals of the known scientific concepts, visitors from another world, horrible mutations of plant or animal life, robots, puzzling natural phenomena for which no satisfactory scientific explanation is known, Frankensteinian experiments, and scores of others. Whichever way he turns, he will still need to observe the fundamental pattern of story-telling, but conflict appears almost inherently in the tale of science-fiction, since any facing of something unknown is in itself conflict.

The usual pattern, however, is quite readily perceived, in so far as the average science-fiction tale is concerned. An inventor invents something and the conflict is established by the invention's getting out of hand. A curious mutation in plant life is discovered and it is found to be carnivorous, preying upon human beings. A meteorite falls to earth and, cooling, spawns a predatory life which is immune to most weapons known to man, or a plague attacks mankind from a meteor or a spaceship from another galaxy. The resolving of the conflict, of course, is the denouement of the story. The pure science-fiction story gets along not only very nicely, but far better, without a love interest—just as most good mysteries do; but some readers demand a love interest, and if editors insist upon it, the novice should have no trouble about including it, since the pseudo-science story pattern does not allow a great deal of variation in its love interest. Generally, the love interest in a science-fiction story is an unwarranted intrusion.

In science-fiction, as well as in other imaginative fiction, some of the best effects are gained by the use of familiar settings and characters. Donald Wandrei, who subscribes to the belief that "dislocations in space and time" are the most profoundly horrible experiences possible to mankind, and who has written many orthodox science-fiction tales, demonstrates in *The Crystal Bullet* that Lovecraft and Wells were right in demanding the familiar setting for their departure from the normal.

The Crystal Bullet is typical of better science-fiction stories. It is simply the story of "something" that falls out of the sky within sight of a farmer in the valley of the Upper Mississippi. He goes curiously to look at it, expecting to find a meteorite. But it was no "shooting-star . . . it resembled the nose of a shell, or a giant bullet, standing two feet high, upon a blackly metallic base; but its fluted sides curved to embrace a tiny filament set in its tip; the object tilted at an angle of nearly forty-five degrees, as though pointing toward its origin in the distant immensities of stars and universe; and its entirety veined with a net-work of fine green threads among the crystal." It seems to him more like a machine, and he observes that "all around it . . . whiteness covered the ground—as hoarfrost" which seemed to come from the greenish light with which the object shone. Stepping into that light, he is aware of deep, terrible cold. Later, he takes the object, despite being almost frozen by it, to his house and puts it on a stump nearby, noting how oddly it swings north-ward towards the region of Polaris, and stands thusly, at a forty-five degree angle. His wife fears it, begs him to take it away, but he believes he should send it down to the state university for the scientists to examine. In the night he awakens to find that his wife has been drawn to the crystal bullet, which has put forth some queer, drawing force; he rescues her, but he is too late—she has frozen to death. He takes the bullet and throws it into the nearby lake, where it shatters and vanishes.

That is the story; there is nothing more to it. But, in its emphasis upon something alien which touched upon and brought tragedy to a young farmer and his wife, *The Crystal Bullet* is almost Fortean in concept, which is to say that, imaginative as it is, the reader is made to believe that it is not at all impossible, such a thing could happen, and is made to remember having read of strange objects having fallen from the sky, etc. Despite the fact that it is not ortho-dox in treatment, *The Crystal Bullet* succeeds very well. It stands at the exact antipodes from Wandrei's *The Red Brain*, which has no contact whatsoever with earth, whereas this story has but one strange and tenuous contact with the extra-terrestrial.

An examination of the prose style of *The Crystal Bullet* indicates that Wandrei tells his story without any contrived drama at all; his prose is straightforward, almost simple, and his story has no concealed climaxes. It is right that it should be so, because Wandrei correctly reasons that his funda-mental theme—two little people facing a mystery out of space and time—presented realistically rather than romanti-cally, is essentially more dramatic than any contrived drama.

The first and the third person narrative style are used with perhaps equal facility and felicitousness in the pseudo-science tale, and, very rarely, the diary form, a variation of the first-person technique, is successfully used. Very probably the success of Bram Stoker's *Dracula* inspired a flood of similarly conceived stories written in the form of a diary, but on the whole, this form is very difficult to do well. That is because the writer is always caught between the necessity of getting on with his story and of keeping a semblance of verisimilitude about the entries as they are likely to be made. A diary may be utilized by many of his readers, and the writer knows very well that successive entries in a diary are not likely to carry a story along without digressions, even when presented as selected entries. Yet the simple demands of good fiction make it imperative that virtually every entry further the story in progress. The author must therefore, if he insists upon using this form, find some ingenious means of keeping his story convincing on the one hand, and of giving it movement on the other. Successive entries in a diary, read even as culled excerpts, are likely to become excessively tiring. Yet, if the writer permits himself to ramble, the diary form may be one of the easiest for him to do. The best method would seem to be to write the story as you feel it should be written in the diary form, and then, once it is finished, to prune carefully to achieve as much movement as possible within the successive entries. Essentially, there is no difference between a diary and a journal for the presentation of a tale of the weird or pseudo-scientific, a diary being primarily about something that happens to the narrator, a journal being a record of events witnessed or apprehended as happening to someone else or in the vicinity of the journalist. Likewise similar in technique and writing problems is the story told in a series of letters. Bram Stoker, it will be noted, utilized diary, letters, and journal in the telling of *Dracula*.

The science-fiction story which succeeds most readily is that which forces the reader's recognition of how fundamentally unstable is man's position in the universe—and how comparatively unimportant. As everyone should know, the slightest alteration in the balance of nature may eliminate mankind from the face of the earth. A new glacial era may do likewise, and so may a general heightening of the temperature, for instance. It does no harm to startle the reader out of his complacence. That was primarily the goal of Charles Fort—not baiting science and scientists, as some critics have seen Fort. But, on the other hand, a great many human minds are simply incapable of accepting or even of contemplating the cosmos at large. A man who is told that if man could travel in one second at the speed of light in a year, it would take him sixteen years to reach the outermost reaches of the "mapped" cosmos, has simply no real comprehension of such space, but he may understand what an incredibly infinitesimal mote he is in the universe.

The science-fiction tale may be said to exist on a different plane from ordinary fiction in that it is not by any means always directed at emphasizing the dignity of man. To the scientist, man is only another creature, representing higher development, to be sure, but one of a race which has risen to great heights in the very short history of earth, and fallen to great depths within that same period of time. The science-fiction writer is neither more nor less than his characters, and his appeal is of course always to his fellow men; whereas the ghost story writer may leave his reader with the feeling that if he is not careful, something of this sort may happen to him, the science-fiction writer is likely to take as his goal the conviction of the reader that if we are all not careful about our natural laws, insofar as it is possible for us to be, something of this kind will certainly happen to us. Science fiction thus divides into two major classes—that in which the human being is inevitably the hero, and the concept of the tale is merely that of superficial conflict with something from outside, leaving the hero, that is "man", to triumph; and that in which man is only an incidental feature on the landscape, and quite as likely to be overcome, and in fact very often destroyed with magnificent impartiality by the forces of nature or by forces subject to other and alien laws in large part beyond the comprehension of the characters of the story. Interplanetary tales and stories of runaway inventions belong in the former class, while alterations of natural laws within the universe belong to the latter.

A magazine like *Astounding Science-Fiction* is open to any kind of good pseudo-scientific tale, whether it is one of galactic travel or one which is highly intellectualized; as long as it is a good story within the boundaries of reader-understanding, it may find a ready market in *Astounding Science-Fiction*, which is perhaps the only market not entirely given over to considerations of the merely entertaining on the level of action fiction, though *Weird Tales* is always hospitable to a good story of pseudo-science and, in fact, no editor in the field today will turn down a first-rate story in the genre, action or not, if he has a free hand. Certain markets by no means exclusively devoted to the field also use science-fiction from time to time, particularly magazines like *Blue Book* and *Adventure,* which has been known to take good super-

natural stories also, having published two of the best uncanny novelettes of the late Reverend Henry S. Whitehead.

Comedy in the tale of pseudo-science is not at all out of
place, and has many times been successfully utilized. Many
readers will remember the series of tales by Edgar Franklin
concerning the wacky inventions of Hawkins, which appeared in the old *Argosy,* and various classics in the field are
well known—H. G. Wells' *The Truth About Pyecraft,* for instance, or Farnsworth Wright's *An Adventure in the Fourth
Dimension,* and Mark Twain's *A Connecticut Yankee in
King Arthur's Court,* which, however much it is primarily
comedy, yet embodies the pseudo-scientific principle. A more
recent novel, *Lest Darkness Fall,* by L. Sprague de Camp,
does very much the same thing, and in his note prefacing his
novel, de Camp frankly admits that *Lest Darkness Fall* is a
story on the Connecticut Yankee theme "about the period
that Toynbee calls the Western Interregnum." De Camp, incidentally, has made a conscious attempt to make the dialogue of his stories completely authentic, though he does introduce contemporary slang on the theory that the people of
the novel's time must have used some. *Lest Darkness Fall*
is eminently successful, but a second novel, *The Incomplete
Enchanter,* by de Camp and Fletcher Pratt, about a mage
who confused his chants and got some amazing results, is
less successful, the device wearing a little thin, and the comedy a little too obviously meant to be wacky.

The Connecticut Yankee theme is admittedly borderline
science-fiction, and so, too, are the Edgar Franklin stories.
To a somewhat similar extent, a majority of the novels of
the popular A. Merritt are also borderline pseudo-science.
The Moon Pool, The Metal Monster, The People of the

Pit are all romantic as well as weird and pseudo-scientific; Merritt's primary interest was always in romance—that is, love—but his stories and novels are more authentic than most of those in his particular classification because his imagination was abetted by a kind of reportorial thoroughness which made it mandatory for him to spend as much time—if not more—on his background as on the primary plot. Certain of his novels, of course, like *Creep, Shadow!,* and *Burn, Witch, Burn,* are primarily straight weirds. The tremendous popularity of Merritt is an interesting phenomenon for the novice in the field to contemplate; Merritt's appeal cut across all generic lines—his supporters are to be found among the devotees of horror, of the supernatural, of the pseudo-scientific, and of the orthodoxly romantic. Before he is ready to specialize, the novice in the imaginative tale would do well to read a few Merritt titles to discover, if possible, just how Merritt put his tales together. Essentially, they are straightforward narratives, with scrupulous attention to the right details of background and character, and a fine, convincing imagination. Merritt's best work remains *The Moon Pool,* and this is also his most popular.

Fundamentally, of course, the pseudo-scientific tale is a fantasy set within circumscribed limits, and in that it stands well apart from pure fantasy.

The Fantastic Story

Pure fantasy is a kind of dream-world fiction which need not adhere to the orthodox short story plot, and which, very often because it does not adhere to the accepted forms of the short story, is not sustained for even the short novel length. It ranges all the way from the prose of Lord Dunsany to the whimsical tales of many contributors to the late, lamented *Unknown Worlds* magazine, a Street & Smith publication under the same aegis as *Astounding Science-Fiction*.

Dunsany's work is in a class rather largely by itself. It grows out of an original folklore and mythology, and is written in what H. P. Lovecraft has described as "crystalline singing prose". In his *Supernatural Horror in Literature,* Lovecraft writes of Dunsany that he "draws with tremendous effectiveness on nearly every body of myth and legend within the circle of European culture, producing a composite or eclectic cycle of fantasy in which Eastern color, Hellenic form, Teutonic sombreness and Celtic wistfulness are so superbly blended that each sustains and supplements the rest without sacrifice of perfect congruity and homogeneity." Dunsany's fantasy strives to achieve beauty rather than terror, though there are some effective tales of terror scattered among his collections, *A Dreamer's Tales, The Book of Wonder, Tales of Three Hemispheres, Fifty-One Tales*— the stories of Slith, the thief, of Hlo-Hlo, the spider-idol, and of the Gibbelins, for instance. But work in the manner of Dunsany enjoys a very limited market, speaking from the point-of-view of the contemporary writer. Even H. P. Lovecraft's fantasies, written under the influence of Dunsany, were little published before his death; it was only after his death that the demand for more of his work brought about their acceptance and publication by editors who had previously rejected them. Of Lovecraft's pure fantasies, only *The White Ship* and *The Strange High House in the Mist* were popular among readers of *Weird Tales*.

But Dunsanian fantasy is only a small portion of the field. The fantasy of beauty is, however, as legitimate as the fantasy of terror, and fully as imaginative. For instance, W. H. Hudson's memorably beautiful story of the bird-girl, Rima, *Green Mansions,* is fantasy of a high order. So too is Lafcadio Hearn's wonderfully beautiful short novel, *Chita,* a book which, after it has once been read, cannot be forgotten, but lingers in memory as the perfume of flowers lingers in a room long after they have been taken away. It is Hearn's prose more than anything else which gives *Chita* the aspect of fantasy, and his way of telling the story, for the story of *Chita* is orthodox enough in essence, and it could very well have happened. It is presumably based on a Creole legend of a child found after a hurricane had separated her family, raised by a childless couple, and ultimately finding her father just prior to his death. But it is a story the telling of which seems to set it in that strange borderland between today and tomorrow, yesterday and today, between life and death, belonging fully to neither, a story of undying retrospect, as it were, which violates many canons of good story-telling and yet emerges as one of the greatest of its kind. That it should impress a reader as fantastic is a tribute to a great stylist, for by fantasy we understand generally a story or a theme which, if not absolutely in the realm of the impossible, is at least highly unlikely. W. H. Hudson's Rima is unlikely, but not impossible, but Hearn's *Chita* is not only possible, but it might have been quite likely, not alone as the basis of a legend.

The story of the lost child is very much akin to the profound dislocation of the life pattern typical of those stories in which a tremendous cataclysm, a plague, or the like eliminates from earth almost all life, and the story is concerned with the struggle of the last man or last woman to survive.

S. Fowler Wright's *Deluge,* for instance, or M. P. Shiel's *The Purple Cloud.* The writer of successful fantasy is usually a man whose prose style is quite superior to that of the average writer; it should be evident at once that this almost inevitably must be so, because it requires exceeding skill to make fantasy convincing. After all, the writer of a ghost story, or a romantic story, or even of an average pseudo-scientific story can call upon a recognizable background to establish a point of contact with his readers; but the writer of fantasy must very often start from scratch, so to speak, with nothing but similarity of emotions between character and reader.

The symbological setting, such as that in *Perelandra,* by C. S. Lewis, is not superficially apparent, because it cannot be, the author having to face the need of establishing his fantastic setting as setting, without concerning himself with indicating his symbolism. Lewis's is primarily always allegorical on a religious theme, and the allegory, as in *Perelandra,* is very soon apparent. What Lewis does, in effect, is to take a religious thesis and emphasize it most entertainingly in a story which, on the surface, is highly fantastic. Fantasy, then, is not the primary interest of the writer, but only the secondary one, the allegory being all-important. But such stories are no less fantastic, for all that; it is perfectly possible to read C. S. Lewis's novels and enjoy them as fantasy without ever becoming aware of their allegorical significance.

The verisimilitude of a setting in which few aspects strike the note of common human experience is quite difficult to achieve. It is one thing for a novice to describe a landscape, a house, a room, a street, upon reading of which the aver-

age reader at once feels at home, drawing upon his own experience to see in his mind's eye just what kind of landscape,
house, room, or street the author intends him to see; but it
is quite another to make real for such an average reader a
world totally dissimilar from anything he has ever seen or
imagined. It may be argued that the average man has never
seen the far corners of the earth, but that is really not an
argument at all, for he has heard of them, he may even have
read of them. A man who has never been to Singapore has
heard about it, even if only by name in a story by Sax
Rohmer, for instance, and it therefore has a certain meaning
to him, he believes in Singapore as a place, and, though he
may have an entirely erroneous picture of it in his mind's
eye, he has already accepted the fundamental fact that Singapore does exist. The writer who employs an utterly alien
setting must utilize every skill he has to make his reader
believe in his setting; a man who lives in a country of trees
and hills will naturally find it a little difficult to "see" in his
mind's eye a country of flat, sandy stretches, without trees
or bushes, and with every evidence of strange flora and fauna.
Yet that is a comparatively trivial parallel when set up along-
side some of the settings employed by contemporary fan-
taisistes.

M. P. Shiel's *The Purple Cloud* is perhaps one of the very
best of all novels of fantasy; certainly it is one which is not
easily thrust from memory, and Shiel's development of the
"last man" theme is very convincingly done. Shiel, of course,
is one of the greatest living stylists writing in English. *The
Purple Cloud* is the story of a curse which comes out of the
arctic to destroy mankind, leaving but one survivor, whose
sensations and experiences as he roams through the corpse-

littered and treasure-strewn places of the world he had known, and now knows as its unchallenged master, are skillfully done and artistically conceived. Shiel's concession to popular taste, however, mitigates to some extent the excellent impression of the first half of the book; for his survivor inevitably finds that he is not alone, but that a woman has also survived, and they can begin all over again. Despite this concession, however, Shiel's Adam Jeffson is a memorable character—but not because he is Adam Jeffson so much as because he is Shiel's character, for Shiel is a writer who has tremendous potency and magic in his prose. His Adam Jeffson, memorable as he is, is not to be compared with his sinister Dr. Krasinski, and the doctor himself is nobody compared to Richard Hogarth of *The Lord of the Sea*, that wildly improbable but magnificently entertaining epitome of all the adventure stories ever written by man.

It is interesting to examine what Shiel has to say for his work, particularly since his style is manifest even in his communications. "Since the object of Art is to enlarge (or at least to sharpen, or at the very least to refresh) your consciousness of the truth of things, the question is, which of the two is the truer, realism or romance? Well, there can be no question that romance is true, if it be truly realistic, but the truth is that it is not truly realistic, if it be not romantic, since truth is romantic. With the mood of wistfulness in your eyes you look at the moon one night where, as musing she walks amid the stars, and wish that you were there where she muses; wait: before you go to bed you will be where she muses, if our globe be moving that way, and soon you may be soaring not at all far from where Venus at this hour leads the crowd of the starry orchestra with her crown and psaltery," he has written. And examine this succinct description: "She was a woman of twenty-five, large and buxom, though neat-waisted, her face beautifully fresh and wholesome, and he of middle-size, with a lazy ease of carriage, small eyes set far apart, a blue-velvet jacket, duck trousers very dirty, held up by a belt, a red shirt, an old cloth hat, a careless carle, greatly famed."

This matter of style is important to the writer of fantasy. Shiel has a sense of swiftness which is far and away beyond the fastest action of a modern hardboiled detective story; what is more, he has the ability to convey movement of the most electrifying sort in a story in which there is no actual physical movement at all! He does it all with words, nothing more, words and their arrangement and a keen sense of word-meanings and values. If you read Shiel, let us say, *The Lord of the Sea* or *The Purple Cloud* or that breathless novel of mystery and detection, *How the Old Woman Got Home,* you are aware, no matter how critical your approach may be, of having an experience, you are pulled, drawn, almost flown along on a gloriously romantic and fantastic journey, you become conscious of a richness you never knew the English language had before, and you think of such trite words as "gorgeous" and "thrilling" and nothing really adequate to convey to your acquaintances or even to yourself just precisely what the effect of all this wild magic of words and sentences and wonderful people and deeds is, or just how it is gained.

The fact is that Shiel at one and the same time over-writes and under-writes; by that I mean to say that he says no more than is absolutely necessary in the barest sense to tell his readers of matters of speech, action, and movement generally

—(he can take you across the city of London as if you were in an aeroplane with an unhampered view on all sides in the space of half a paragraph)—and he permits himself to expand when the matter is one of sensuous imagery, of color, for instance, of scene, emotional experience, and all things pertaining to the senses. In this lies his effect, but admittedly mine is a barren summary, an explanation not entirely satisfactory, because Shiel is still more than this. Arthur Machen, too, is a stylist in more sombre colors, and Dunsany—in more consciously beautiful language based on Biblical phraseology.

Style is important to the writer because it means a great deal to the reader even if the reader is not aware of it as style at all. A style of one's own is developed only with time and writing experience, and sometimes not at all. It is too easy to imitate a style or styles, or to content one's self with simple prose and dialogue and emphasize story above everything else. But even simplicity has its mannerisms, and the use of words and phrases and sentences is very important in achieving an effect. That this should be true in fantasy more than in any other kind of writing ought to be obvious; it is because, as I have written earlier, the fantastic setting needs more than the prosaic in language to be made convincing. It is all very well to catalog, which is to say, to write in such a manner that your description becomes only a catalog of contents, as for instance:

The rather barren room contained only two chairs, a table, a picture hung askew, and a broken pedestal, on which stood a bowl of colored water or glass, through which the sun shone.

Certainly it is all there, pat, and precise. Try it this way:

> The only light in the room came through the half
> opened window where the sunlight straggled in and sho
> through a bowl of green-colored water or glass, and
> from there was diffused about the room in a soft, emer
> ald radiance which fell impartially upon two chairs and
> a table, and rather more reluctantly, it seemed, on an
> indistinct picture hung crookedly on the wall away from
> the door and window both. At any moment, it seemed,
> the broken pedestal upon which the bowl stood, might
> fall, but it did not, it sustained the bowl, and the bowl
> sustained the sunlight, and the diffused, strange green
> light in turn sustained and gave life to an otherwise
> barren room.

The room has not had a stick of furniture added, clearly; but something more has got into it just the same. The cataloging of appurtenances has its place; but its place is not very often in the fantastic story.

But style does not consist in the use of unusual or florid words; it does not consist in thickly-strewn adjectives; it does not grow out of turgidity; style is something substantially constructed, not studied, something that flows easily and comes only from long practise. It is important to learn to write just enough and no more; many an apple has been spoiled by being cooked too much or too little, so to speak. A writer almost never consciously sets out to develop a style; this comes, given time and the will to write—and the writing. It is not only possible but advisable for the young writer who is interested in this matter of style to study a textbook or two on the subject, and to examine the evolution of a stylist's prose manner from his first to his later books.

The field of the fantastic story actually knows no boundaries except the mundane. Fantasy may be the vehicle of a delightful farce or satire. In the past decade at least two writers have been very successful with novels about miracles—Bruce Marshall with *Father Malachy's Miracle,* and Edwin Greenwood's *Miracle in the Drawing Room.* The former is more widely known, because it has been both dramatized and filmed. Its theme is quite simple—a sincere, simple-hearted priest manages to have a miracle performed, but the miracle poses a knotty problem since it a) inconveniences a number of people; b) is unorthodox; c) ought not to have been done at all without the proper authority; and the upshot of the whole matter is that the priest effects another miracle to undo the first. Now this is fantasy of a high order; true, it is primarily a satire, but its entire action depends upon the unfortunate priest's miracle, brought about solely as a point of faith.

This kind of fantasy has a satisfactory audience. So too has a book like Maude Meagher's *Fantastic Traveler,* which is all about David Martin, who took refuge in his imagination from the workaday world and had dreams more wonderful than any ever had by an opium-eater, and, to a lesser extent, because it is a relatively crude performance beside *Fantastic Traveler,* has Thomas Calvert McClary's *Rebirth,* which is based upon the assumption that at a certain hour one day all people forgot everything they knew, and had to begin over with intelligence and ability to think, without memory, customs, habits, etc., a novel idea and one not done too often in any form. E. M. Forster's famous *The Celestial Omnibus,* driven by Sir Thomas Browne and Dante, which carried a lad who loved beauty and a man who prated about it from here to yonder, among the immortals, is likewise fantasy of a high order.

The variations are virtually unlimited. Such popular novels as Oscar Wilde's *The Picture of Dorian Gray* and David Garnett's *Lady Into Fox* stand side by side with such less-known novels as Olaf Stapledon's *Sirius* and Arthur Mac-Arthur's *After the Afternoon.* The symbolical theme of a portrait's representing an aging human soul while the body of its possessor stays young and untouched by time and dissipation (*The Picture of Dorian Gray*), the delightful whimsy of a lady's becoming a fox (*Lady Into Fox*), the amusing parable of an educated and sensitive dog (*Sirius*), and the Grecian tale of a faun, lover of Aphrodite, who had the power to enter any human body of his choice (*After the Afternoon*) are all alike fantastic, and legitimate stories of fantasy.

One of the most widely-loved books of all time is allegorical fantasy—Lewis Carroll's *Alice in Wonderland;* and one of the most pungent and philosophical of books, broadly mocking a great many beliefs of famous people, is likewise fantasy—Charles Erskine Scott Wood's *Heavenly Discourse.* Any lover of fantasy who has not yet read G. K. Chesterton's *The Man Who Was Thursday* has a treat in store for him. An increasing taste for sheer whimsy has followed *Lady Into Fox,* and come to its fullest flower in tales of a man who could fly (*The Flying Yorkshireman* and *Sam Small Flies Again,* by Eric Knight), a letter-carrier who slowly turned into a tree (*Mr. Sycamore,* by Robert Ayre), and a man-fish (*The Man-Fish of North Creek,* by Tronby Fenstad). The man-fish story, of course, belongs to the province of folk-lore, as do a great many other tales in the early years of American letters, from Washington Irving's *Rip Van Winkle* to the anonymously invented adventures of Paul Bunyan, Mike Fink, John Henry, Pecos Bill, and a handful of other American folk heroes, all essentially regional Americana. No one has succeeded so well with the fantastic recounting of American folk lore, to which he has added delightful whimsy and color and inventive genius peculiarly his own, as the late Stephen Vincent Benét, whose *The Devil and Daniel Webster* particularly has already become an accepted part of the best in American legend. Some of the best whimsical fantasy by contemporary writers has been gathered into two notable anthologies, which the would-be writer should not miss— *Two Bottles of Relish*, edited by Whit Burnett (1943), and *Pause to Wonder*, edited by Marjorie Fischer and Rolfe Humphries (1944).

Fantasy and comedy often go hand in hand. That series of collaborations called the "Chester-Bellocs" contains at least one hilariously funny satire which it would be instructive for both readers and writers of the fantastic story to read; it is *The Haunted House*. The Sam Small tales are primarily funny, and so are such tales as that of the languishing lady upon whom a camel came to call (*The Camel*, by Lord Berners, in *Two Bottles of Relish*), and the recent fantasy by Eric Linklater, *The Wind on the Moon*, the story of Dinah and Dorinda and their career of misconduct when the wind is on the moon.

It should be observed also that the realm of fantasy is particularly appropriate for juvenile fiction, if the writer is inclined to try his hand for one of the most critical segments of the American reading public. A great deal of juvenile fiction is fantastic in character, and much of this fantasy is ex-

tremely popular. One has only to think of the *Pooh* book
by A. A. Milne and of the *Mary Poppins* books by Pamela
Travers. Writing fantasy for the juvenile audience has one
advantage over that for the adult reader—the juvenile reader
or listener is not likely to balk at accepting any setting, no
matter how strange—but strangeness of setting and prose
style will not make up for an ineffective story insofar as the
juvenile reader is concerned.

Once the novice at writing has determined to enter the
field of fantasy, and has familiarized himself with outstanding works in the field, he will find his greatest difficulty in
avoiding outright imitation. He can hardly avoid influence;
the imaginative concepts of writers in the genre are usually
potent enough and powerfully enough presented to take hold
of the imagination very markedly, and it requires a special
effort to shake one's self free of their dominance, particularly
if one is at work with the same tools. Even influence ought
to be avoided as much as possible, though it may be very
difficult at first. The writer who writes a great deal may not
even be aware of influences at work in his efforts. It was not
until I had put together my first collection of weird tales
(*Someone in the Dark*, 1941) and had grouped the stories
that I saw clearly that the three groups had been moulded
by the work of three past masters—Montague Rhodes
James, Mary E. Wilkins-Freeman, and H. P. Lovecraft—
though I had done the last-named group of stories in deliberate imitation of Lovecraft's manner in combination with my
own lesser additions at Lovecraft's behest, repeatedly made
before his death; and, having seen it, I was bound to ac-
knowledge this influence in my introduction to that volume.

Avoiding influences and dominations yet remains second

ry to avoiding the mundane; the writer of fantasy who is not possessed of a strong and vivid imagination had better raise his standards in another field. A vivid and colorful imagination is vitally necessary to the writer of fantasy, an imagination which the prosaic desiderata of every-day life cannot affect in any telling way. Secondarily, a keen sensibility for the shadings of the meaning and color of words and phrases, and an assured skill in putting them together, coupled with a good story sense, are necessary—unless he is determined to write in the field of pure fantasy and eschew the possibility of much remuneration from his efforts. Of all the avenues open to the writer of imaginative fiction, the fantastic story offers the widest basic variety, as distinct from the tale of ghosts, of pseudo-science, and various other types within the boundaries of the imagination.

Other Gambits

Within the past two decades there has been a strongly marked increase in interest in a type of mystery novel usually described as of "psychological horror", and rather more in the province of imaginative fiction than in that of the romantic, though it combines both the elements of imagination and of romance. The novel of psychological horror may be an orthodox detective story, like that chilling tale, *Death Walks in Eastrepps,* by Francis Beeding, or Ethel Lina White's *Wax;* it may be a novel of pure horror, like Virginia Swain's *The Hollow Skin,* or something as strange and indescribable as Charles Williams's *The Place of the Lion;* and it may be a study of murder and madness like Chris Massie's *The Green Circle.* Whatever its sub-classifications, it is always a study in suspense and terror.

The imaginative writer, far more than any other, must be a master of suspense; he must be able to make a reader find it virtually impossible to wait to turn the page and find out what happens next; he must be able to quicken his reader's pulse and give him that uncomfortable feeling that he is no longer alone at his reading; he must, in short, have the skill to put his reader into the precise difficulty of the hero. Certain writers, like Ethel Lina White, Joseph Shearing (a nom-de-plume for Marjorie Bowen), Francis Iles, Dorothy B. Hughes, and others, have this skill to a very high degree of excellence among the more popular contemporary writers, and as apart from the writers in the field who are more concerned with detection than with suspense and terror.

For, primarily, the novel of psychological horror, except when it is frankly supernatural, is within the domain of the detective story. Very often its chief character is a detective, and the reader may need to follow him through the case. But in most novels of psychological horror or terror, the detective is secondary, and the character who is experiencing the terror is the leading character with whom the reader identifies himself. There is, then, a certain difference between the orthodox novel of detection and the novel of psychological horror, even though the solution of crime may be the motivating factor in both.

The orthodox detective story at its best is akin to a mathematical problem on the same plane as a puzzle in chess. It inevitably follows a set pattern—a crime is committed, the detective is called, the crime is investigated and solved, sometimes from an armchair, sometimes with a great deal of tearing around and a lot of violent action. This fundamental pattern holds true whether the sleuth is C. Auguste Dupin, Sherlock Holmes, or Dr. John Thorndyke on one hand, or Lord Peter Wimsey, Hildegarde Withers, Ellery Queen, or Nero Wolfe on the other. The puzzle is a challenge to the reader, the reading of the story is a contest between the author and the reader, and the result, one way or the other, is usually always felicitous. It is a kind of adventurous romance in which the reader takes a very definite and active part not only by identifying himself with the investigation, but by trying to beat it to the solution. At its second best, the detective story is complicated by a love interest and— well, let us just say, other considerations.

Curiously enough, the same reader who is entirely likely to raise his voice in protest if a love interest shows up in his problem in deduction, takes a love interest in the novel of psychological horror in his stride, provided that it is kept properly secondary to the suspense and terror which are manifestly the initial concern of the novel in the genre. All these novels have a certain macabre fascination. Their technique permits of some wider variation than that of the orthodox detective story, whether one of deduction or one of action. It embraces the story told by the criminal as well as the victim, the story narrated by the innocent bystander who is innocently drawn into the crime or intrigue or whatever it is that sets in motion the web of terror which presently enmeshes the reader as well as the characters in the book; it may be a story put together from various documents pertaining to the case; it may be a fine, realistic study in the morbid psychology of murder based on true crimes, as are all the novels of Joseph Shearing, for instance, presented with such fidelity that one wonders repeatedly whether they ought not to be put into the domain of the realistic story, for they are real stories in one sense, and in another they are only real cases which have been sifted through the mind of a singularly brilliant writer.

The innocent bystander theme has been especially popular in the novel of terror, and Ethel Lina White has done this very well in *The Wheel Spins* and other, similar novels; H. Russell Wakefield did it in *Hearken to the Evidence,* which was a deliberate attempt to write a novel primarily about people caught in a murder investigation and thus has kinship with Gerald Bullett's remarkable *The Jury,* likewise a realistic work treating of the members of the jury at a murder trial. Very probably the innocent bystander theme is popular because it is very much easier to identify yourself as a reader with an "innocent bystander" than with someone deliberately concerned; moreover, it is essentially more terrible to most readers that an "innocent" person (by which is meant someone innocent of any guilt in connection with the actual crime) should be involved, than that someone who might somehow be connected to it should be, the reader, of course, inevitably identifying himself with the blamelessness—which may be regarded by the novice at realistic writing as evidence of delightful naïveté. Nevertheless, it is true—the reader is the innocent bystander, and his participation is required to fulfil the intentions of the author in writing the novel. The novel on this theme usually progresses thenceforth with increasing suspense and terror through a series of baffling and utterly terrifying events to its revelatory conclusion, though occasionally the author leaves some very neat questions, and the reader must arrive at his own decisions in regard to the events about which he has been reading—as in R. C. Ashby's *He Arrived at Dusk.*

One of the very best themes utilized in both the short and the long lengths is that of the vanished woman, now so common that it keeps cropping up in the newspapers as a "news" story from time to time, which is to say that it has reached the status of legend, and now and then some enterprising reporter hears it and duly makes a story of it. The theme is simple: a young woman and her companion (mother, aunt, or governess) arrive at a Parisian hotel at a time when some great Exposition (peace conference, etc.) is going on, and take a room. The elder lady is indisposed, the hotel doctor is sent for, declares her condition serious, and dispatches the girl on an errand of some duration, usually after medicine for her mother. After an agonizing time, the girl returns to the hotel—but there the house manager, the desk clerk, the doctor who had sent her off all declare that they do not know her; she demands to be shown up to the room where she left her mother; she is taken up—there is the room, number and all—but beyond the door!—even the wallpaper is different, and someone else occupies it. Her mother has simply vanished, and the poor distraught girl is almost driven insane before the solution of the mystery turns up; it is simply that the elder woman had managed to bring to Paris a case of the black plague, of which she had died, and, rather than permit publication of an obituary containing that fact and so scatter the people who had gathered for the Exposition, all the people concerned at the hotel, together with the police of the district, were joined in a conspiracy to prevent its publication by simply obliterating all trace of the unfortunate victim. The story has turned up in altered form in at least two good novels of the genre: Mrs. Belloc-Lowndes' *The End of Her Honeymoon,* and Lawrence Rising's *She Who Was Helena Cass,* and in several short stories by various hands.

The fundamental situation is one of peculiar terror. It is actually, in effect, a profound dislocation, and no one can fail to be moved by the terror of the poor young woman who is so blandly denied recognition by everyone to whom she had spoken in Paris, and treated as if she were out of her mind. This story is pre-Freudian in origin, it need hardly be pointed out. Perhaps the devotees of the psychoanalysis and psychiatry which followed Freud might have made something quite different out of it. Insanity and psychoses of various kinds have become the mainstay of many novelists in the genre. There is a brooding horror of homicidal mania about Beeding's *Death Walks in Eastrepps,* the mass-murders in which are particularly well done, designed to inspire the utmost horror in the reader, and succeeding very well. Mental derangements abound in the same author's later book, *The House of Dr. Edwardes,* filmed as *Spellbound* not long ago. Then there is Hugh Walpole's story of the demented man who experimented with pain on human beings, *Portrait of a Man with Red Hair;* and that is to say nothing of another Hugh Walpole tale, *The Killer and the Slain,* which reverses the well known formula in Robert Louis Stevenson's *Dr. Jekyll and Mr. Hyde,* which featured two opposing personalities in one body, by dividing one personality between two men, so that when one killed the other he killed himself as well. And there is Hugh Brooke's fine study of insanity, *The Web,* far too little known in this country, though it was published over here in 1934. Most recent of the studies in pathology which have achieved a steadily mounting success is *The Green Circle,* by Chris Massie, the story of Egan Bothwick, a brilliant student who attempts murder and goes insane because of an unhappy love affair, the significance of the title lying in a green Christmas ball, suspended in the window of his beloved's house, which appears constantly in various forms to his disordered mind.

Manifestly, the writer who would attempt the psychological horror novel in the pathology division must have special knowledge. It is far simpler, even if it requires no less writing skill, to deal with unreconstructed evil in persons or places, as in Russell Thorndike's fine novel, *The Devil in the Belfry,* or Francis Brett Young's *Cold Harbour,* or Leonard Cline's *The Dark Chamber* or Herbert Gorman's *The Place Called Dagon.* The evil house gambit is particularly a favorite. It has been done in combination with sorcery in Evangeline Walton's *Witch House,* and with abnormal psychology in Craig Rice's *Telefair,* with a malevolent revenant in Daphne du Maurier's *Rebecca,* with the psychic residue of an old crime in Helen Irvine's *77 Willow Road,* and so on. This sort of approach is considerably easier to make, though it requires no less skill, and it needs besides a potent descriptive power. The brooding and terrible forces in the house of Dorothy Macardle's *The Uninvited,* for instance, are not brought to reality by a simple statement of their existence. No, as in all such cases, the author must make his reader feel them and see them and sense them in every way before a name is put to them. In the majority of cases of evil houses, however, the disturbing or occupying force is primarily supernatural and thus comes under the head of the ghost story, rather than of the psychological horror tale.

Madness of any kind is very difficult to convey. It is especially so, of course, in a realistic novel, the reader of which must have every step clearly before him. In writing about the growing madness of the Countess Eleanor Brogmar in *Restless Is the River*, I had to face the dilemma of whether to delineate her condition in sympathetic detail and be accused of longwindedness, or whether to touch upon the successive stages of her madness as little as possible and be accused of being unconvincing by the critics. I decided in favor of verisimilitude, and portrayed her madness painstakingly. The irony of it was, as one might expect, that I was duly accused of both longwindedness and lack of conviction, but I had the satisfaction of receiving many letters from doctors and nurses connected with institutions for the care of the insane testifying to the accuracy of my portrait, which, as the evidence of people who had to deal with insanity directly, seemed to me far more valuable than the mere opinions of critics who lacked special knowledge of the subject which they presumed to judge.

The problem is not quite so difficult for romantic or imaginative work, since the reader who turns to either is conditioned to accept more for granted than the reader of a realistic novel. Yet that is not an excuse for the writer in the field to be at all careless about his material; he owes himself the most meticulous writing he can do, apart from the "precious," and he owes no less to his reader. It is true that less words are required for a frankly imaginative or romantic story, but no less care need be exercised. The fact is that insanity as a subject is difficult to make convincing no matter in what form of fiction it occurs; madness is repugnant and alien to most readers, though it has much the same fascination that the recountings of true crimes do. Madness alone in-

spires horror that is always a mixture of pity, which is pro-
portionate to the kind of madness portrayed—usually very
great in the case of that kind of arteriosclerotic enfeeblement
of the mind so common in senility to very small in the case
of megalomania or homicidal mania.

The megalomaniac very often is portrayed as a straight
criminal, with no suggestion of the abnormal. Dr. Krasinski
of M. P. Shiel's *Dr. Krasinski's Secret,* Eustace Skyrme of
Douglas G. Browne's *Plan XVI,* the sinister intriguers of
Réné Hansard's *The Silver Fox,* the insidious and memorably
sadistic *Dr. Fu Manchu*—and all similar arch-criminals are
given to readers straight by and large, though it must be observed that many of them—certainly Krasinski, Skyrme, and
Dr. Fu Manchu—are very definitely on the abnormal side,
and potential case histories in psychiatry. The writer who is
interested in creating this kind of criminal is rather on the
safe side than not by presenting him as an arch- or super-
criminal, since as such he is far more credible to the mass
reader than he would be in psychiatric terms. The problem is
a simple one of having to decide how best to achieve social
resonance, to communicate with the reader; reality is not
involved. Reality, in any case, is far more romantic on occasion—as M. P. Shiel has pointed out—than romance. The
constant presentation of Hitler as a megalomaniac might very
well be construed as an "excuse" for the folly of those who
permitted his rise and his criminal career in the face of everything he had written that he meant to do in his book, *Mein
Kampf,* and even after he began, one by one, to do those
things; the average reader of the penny-dreadful might well
ask how it was that statesmen and politicians did not recognize the typical arch-criminal type when they saw him; dub-

bing him a megalomaniac (as of course he was) may quite possibly remove a little of the onus.

The writer need make no excuses for avoiding the psychiatric, not only because he is not thoroughly versed in it, but because the majority of his potential audience may not know whereof he speaks, and, if this is true, his work will have a limited audience. The novice who has any doubt about questions like this may fall back upon several simple rules. A work of fiction designed as entertainment is not a place to reveal an author's erudition. The more erudite and difficult a work of fiction is, the more difficult it will be, by that same proportion, for the average reader. What a writer has to say should be said as directly as possible, always allowing for the proper verisimilitude of setting and character. Unless a writer can convey psychiatric situations and states of mind clearly, without room for doubt, it is much better to avoid them. This directive should apply to every subject about which there may be doubt in the mind of the author.

Imaginative fiction allows the writer every leeway except one—he ought not to misconstrue or misrepresent the known facts of history, unless he is writing a novel which begins with the fundamental premise that if any chosen event in history had not taken place precisely as it had, what might have happened? It seems hardly necessary to point this out, but writers are too likely to take mere cautionary rules too literally. There are fewer taboos about the writing of imaginative fiction than about the writing of any other type, even though the patterns of arch-criminals, ghosts, horrors, etc., are rather well standardized. There have been some interesting variants, particularly those which have seen the light of day in *Unknown Worlds*, stories like P. Schuyler Miller's

Over the River from that magazine, and Robert Bloch's *Yours Truly, Jack the Ripper,* and H. P. Lovecraft's *The Outsider* from *Weird Tales,* in each one of which the werewolf, the famous unknown criminal, and the lich respectively tells its own story with fair concealment until the climax is reached. Apart from a distracting flipness in Bloch's tale, these stories command respect for originality; so does Frank Belknap Long's tale, *The Refugees,* from *Unknown Worlds,* which concerns elves who have taken refuge in America from war-torn Europe; and so, too, Theodore Sturgeon's *It,* again from *Unknown Worlds,* the terrible story of what rose into life from the remains of one long dead.

The variant is usually interesting, and the writing of it usually a greater challenge to skill, because the reader who is accustomed to set patterns in the fiction of the imaginative, needs a little more good writing to force his acceptance of divagations from those patterns. Variants, however, should not transgress the known or accepted bounds of the subject. Even superstitions exist within fairly standardized frames. If lycanthrophy is the subject chosen by the author, it would not do at all to have the werewolf change come about at high noon, when all the available literature on the subject indicates that the malign change is dependent on the phases of the moon, and is nocturnal. If vampirism is the theme, the reader should be aware of the fact that one bitten by a vampire does not become a vampire unless she dies, according to vampire lore, as a result of such bites; he ought not, therefore, to present the opposite picture. The accepted lore is enough of a problem for the beginner to make convincing to his readers without the addition of any contradictory variants.

Generally speaking, however, the writer in the genre is o
perfectly safe grounds if he swings forthrightly off into th
imagination, with just enough contact with reality to con
vince the reader. However fantastic the concept, the theme
the story, lend it enough verisimilitude and then give it rei
to carry you where it will. But if the writer is new to th
genre, he ought first of all to familiarize himself thoroughl
with the best work in the field, and to that end should rea
widely among anthologies particularly, to acquaint himsel
with the wide variety possible under the heading of "imagina
tive fiction".

A Reading List

Anthologies

SHUDDERS, edited by Lady Cynthia Asquith (1929)

THE GHOST BOOK, edited by Lady Cynthia Asquith (1927)

SPEAK OF THE DEVIL, edited by C. B. Boutell and Sterlin
North (1945)

TWO BOTTLES OF RELISH, edited by Whit Burnett (1943)

FAMOUS GHOST STORIES, edited by Bennett Cerf (1943)

WORLD'S GREAT MYSTERY STORIES, edited by Will Cupp
(1943)

THEY WALK AGAIN, edited by Colin de la Mare (1931)

SLEEP NO MORE, edited by August Derleth (1944)

WHO KNOCKS?, edited by August Derleth (1946)

PAUSE TO WONDER, edited by Marjorie Fischer and Rolf
Humphries (1944)

THE GHOST STORY OMNIBUS, edited by Joseph Lewis Frencl
(1943)

THE SLEEPING AND THE DEAD: 30 UNCANNY TALES, edite
by Stephen Grendon (1946)

CREEPS BY NIGHT, edited by Dashiell Hammett (1931)
BEWARE AFTER DARK!, edited by T. Everett Harré (1929)
TALES OF TERROR, edited by Boris Karloff (1943)
THE KARLOFF READER, edited by Boris Karloff (1945)
THE HAUNTED OMNIBUS, edited by Alexander Laing (1937)
DEVIL STORIES, edited by Maximilian Rudwin (1921)
THE OMNIBUS OF CRIME, edited by Dorothy L. Sayers, (1929)
THE SECOND OMNIBUS OF CRIME, edited by Dorothy L. Sayers (1931)
THE THIRD OMNIBUS OF CRIME, edited by Dorothy L. Sayers (1935)
THE MIDNIGHT READER, edited by Philip van Doren Stern (1942)
THE MOONLIGHT TRAVELER, edited by Philip van Doren Stern (1943)
THE OTHER WORLDS (25 MODERN STORIES OF MYSTERY AND IMAGINATION), edited by Phil Stong (1941)
THE SUPERNATURAL OMNIBUS, edited by Montague Summers (1932)
SIX NOVELS OF THE SUPERNATURAL, edited by Edward Wagenknecht (1944)
GREAT TALES OF TERROR AND THE SUPERNATURAL, edited by Herbert A. Wise and Phyllis Fraser (1944)
PORTABLE NOVELS OF SCIENCE, edited by Donald A. Wollheim (1945)
THE POCKET-BOOK OF SCIENCE-FICTION, edited by Donald A. Wollheim (1943)

Short Stories

TALES BEFORE MIDNIGHT, by Stephen Vincent Benét (1939)
THIRTEEN O'CLOCK, by Stephen Vincent Benét (1937)

THE ROOM IN THE TOWER AND OTHER STORIES, by E. F. Benson (1929)

VISIBLE AND INVISIBLE, by E. F. Benson (1923)

THE LIGHT INVISIBLE, by Robert Benson (1917)

IN THE MIDST OF LIFE, by Ambrose Bierce (1927)

CAN SUCH THINGS BE?, by Ambrose Bierce (1924)

STRANGE STORIES, by Algernon Blackwood (1929)

THE TALES OF ALGERNON BLACKWOOD (1938)

THE DOLL AND ONE OTHER, by Algernon Blackwood (1945)

THE LAST BOUQUET, by Marjorie Bowen (1933)

NIGHT PIECES, by Thomas Burke (1936)

THE KING IN YELLOW, by Robert W. Chambers (1902)

PRESENTING MOONSHINE, by John Collier (1941)

THE TOUCH OF NUTMEG, by John Collier (1943)

THE RIDDLE AND OTHER TALES, by Walter de la Mare (1930)

THE CONNOISSEUR AND OTHER STORIES, by Walter de la Mare (1926)

SOMETHING NEAR, by August Derleth (1945)

A WINTER'S TALES, by Isak Dinesen (1944)

SEVEN GOTHIC TALES, by Isak Dinesen (1934)

THE CONAN DOYLE STORIES (1929)

THE BOOK OF WONDER, by Lord Dunsany (1918)

THE TRAVEL TALES OF MR. JOSEPH JORKENS, by Lord Dunsany (1931)

THE CELESTIAL OMNIBUS, by E. M. Forster (1923)

THE BEAST WITH FIVE FINGERS AND OTHER TALES, by W. F. Harvey (1928)

THE GREAT FOG AND OTHER WEIRD TALES, by H. F. Heard (1944)

Novels

HE ARRIVED AT DUSK, by R. C. Ashby (1933)

MISS HARGREAVES, by Frank Baker (1941)

THE DARK CHAMBER, by Leonard Cline (1927)

LEST DARKNESS FALL, by L. Sprague de Camp (1941)

THE RETURN, by Walter de la Mare (1922)

THE LOST WORLD, by Arthur Conan Doyle (1912)

REBECCA, by Daphne du Maurier (1939)

THE WORM OUROBOROS, by E. R. Eddison (1926)

A MIRROR FOR WITCHES, by Esther Forbes (1928)

STRANGERS IN THE VLY, by Edmund Gilligan (1941)

THE PLACE CALLED DAGON, by Herbert Gorman (1927)

MIRACLE IN THE DRAWING-ROOM, by Edwin Greenwood (1936)

AYESHA, by H. Rider Haggard (1923)

THE SILVER FOX, by Réné Hansard (1938)

CHITA, by Lafcadio Hearn (1889)

THE UNDYING MONSTER, by Jessie Douglas Kerruish (1936)

THE CADAVER OF GIDEON WYCK, by Alexander Laing (1934)

UNCLE SILAS, by J. Sheridan Le Fanu (1926)

OUT OF THE SILENT PLANET, by C. S. Lewis (1943)

THE LURKER AT THE THRESHOLD, by H. P. Lovecraft and August Derleth (1945)

THE UNINVITED, by Dorothy Macardle (1942)

FATHER MALACHY'S MIRACLE, by Bruce Marshall (1931)

THE GREEN CIRCLE, by Chris Massie (1943)

DOCTOR FOGG, by Norman Matson (1929)

REBIRTH, by Thomas Calvert McClary (1944)

FANTASTIC TRAVELER, by Maude Meagher (1931)

THE AMBER WITCH, by Wilhelm Meinhold (1928)

THE MOON POOL, by A. Merritt (1944)

THE SURVIVOR, by Dennis Parry (1940)
TELEFAIR, by Craig Rice (1942)
BROOD OF THE WITCH-QUEEN, by Sax Rohmer (1924)
THE MASTER OF THE MICROBE, by Robert W. Service (1926)
THE SECOND DELUGE, by Garett P. Serviss (1912)
THE HOPKINS MANUSCRIPT, by R. C. Sherriff (1939)
THE PURPLE CLOUD, by M. P. Shiel (1930)
THE LORD OF THE SEA, by M. P. Shiel (1901)
HOW THE OLD WOMAN GOT HOME, by M. P. Shiel (1928)
TO WALK THE NIGHT, by William Sloane (1937)
THE EDGE OF RUNNING WATER, by William Sloane (1939)
THE LADY WHO CAME TO STAY, by R. E. Spencer (1931)
STAR MAKER, by Olaf Stapledon (1927)
SIRIUS, by Olaf Stapledon (1944)
LAST AND FIRST MEN, by Olaf Stapledon (1934)
THE CROCK OF GOLD, by James Stephens (1928)
DRACULA, by Bram Stoker (1924)
THE HOLLOW SKIN, by Virginia Swain (1938)
THE GOLD TOOTH, by John Taine (1927)
THE DEVIL IN THE BELFRY, by Russell Thorndike (1932)
THE OLD LADIES, by Hugh Walpole (1924)
PORTRAIT OF A MAN WITH RED HAIR, by Hugh Walpole
    (1940)
WITCH HOUSE, by Evangeline Walton (1945)
LOLLY WILLOWES, by Sylvia Townsend Warner (1943)
SEVEN FAMOUS NOVELS, by H. G. Wells (1934)
THE SWORD IN THE STONE, by T. H. White (1939)
THE WITCH IN THE WOOD, by T. H. White (1939)
THE PLACE OF THE LION, by Charles Williams (1932)
NIGHT UNTO NIGHT, by Philip Wylie (1944)
COLD HARBOUR, by Francis Brett Young (1925)

IV: MARGINAL NOTES

On the Stream-of-Consciousness Method

Though he would be well advised to avoid the stream-of-consciousness method until he is sure of himself, except for experimental purposes in work not meant for publication, the beginner in writing might profit by a study of it. It is, briefly and simply reduced, an extension of the monologue method. The so-called monologue method is the telling of a story in a) straight monologue, that is, one-sided conversation; b) straightforward thought process. Dorothy Parker utilizes this method very ably in several of her stories, particularly *Lady with a Lamp, Sentiment, The Little Hours,* etc. The story is usually perfectly direct, though a good deal of extra wordage is necessary to set off character and background.

The stream-of-consciousness method varies in attempting to reproduce precisely or almost precisely the various things of which the human mind is conscious. Now, as every writer is aware, in man's waking hours he is conscious of a great many uncorrelated and not necessarily to be correlated things, sometimes sharply, sometimes distantly; thoughts flash up, impressions occur, thoughts fade out or are replaced by others not connected; direct sentences, parts of sentences, and so forth are reflected in the mind, similar to a man talking to himself. Manifestly, this sort of thing needs to be done with great skill, or else it becomes a mere hodge-podge sort of catalog, not at all coherent, the reproduction of which, however faithful to reality, lacks social resonance, and is therefore not worthy of publication. The unrelated thoughts, desires, hopes, ambitions, etc., of an individual do inform the reader of his thoughts and thought-patterns, but do little, save in the hands of a very skillful writer, to further a story.

Various novels and short stories in the methods are readily available to the reader, but perhaps the most rewarding are the novels of the late Virginia Woolf, particularly *Mrs. Dalloway, To the Lighthouse,* and *The Years,* and the long, Proustian novel, *Pilgrimage,* by Dorothy Richardson, though Proust's monumental work, *Remembrance of Things Past,* is not a stream-of-consciousness work.

The classic example of the successful stream-of-consciousness method is the meditation of Mrs. Bloom which closes James Joyce's *Ulysses*—almost fifty pages without a punctuation break. Regardless of the difficulty of reading, it is eminently clear to the careful reader. The lack of punctuation is not necessarily a factor in the stream-of-consciousness manner. The disjointed thoughts and desires and observations may or may not be punctuated, and usually are unless the manner is very largely in the form of a monologue, as is Mrs. Bloom's, making a steady, if rambling process from one point to another. The method is on the whole too difficult, involving too much soul-struggle and the temptation to mimic rather than to create, and the results too ineffective and meagre to warrant the use of the stream-of-consciousness method. Even the skilled hand employs it sparingly. It is, obviously, the epitome of the subjective, and the beginner at writing has all he can do with mere objective narrative without turning his hand to something as involved as this. It will

not be amiss, however, for him to acquaint himself with both
the monologue and the pot-pourri forms of stream-of-consciousness writing, and to learn how very effectively small
portions of such writing can be interpolated into an objective
story from time to time. He may find it good exercise simply
to attempt to put down what passes through his mind, though
he will not long be able to do so because he will become involved in the mechanics of so doing, which is to say that he
will become too conscious of what he is doing to long sustain
validity.

On Taking Issue with Editors

It ought not to be thought, simply because it is safe to
assume that editors are right in the majority of times (often
as much from the purely creative point of view as from that
of their considerations for the mass-reader), that a writer is
bound to accept the editor's criticisms at face value. All criticisms ought to be challenged, at least within the author's
mind, and carefully examined; wholesale acceptance is as
bad for the writer as wholesale rejection, implying too little
ego as against too much. Editorial criticism, except when it
is plainly made from the perspective of reader-reaction from
a known audience, is no different in this respect from any
other, no matter by whom offered.

Many a beginner is apt to become discouraged in the face
of criticism, or repeated rejections, unaware that many factors motivate acceptance or rejection of any given manuscript. I have already outlined what I call the "shock-ab-
sorber" practise, which is designed to save the author's ego
from repeated attacks, and does succeed very well. I suggest also that it ought to be clear to a writer that not only is

ego something different from conceit, but that every writer ought to have a healthy ego (not necessarily an obtrusive one), and he ought to take good care of it. Reduced to its simplest terms, ego is the impelling force in a creative urge, and the sustaining principle. It enables a writer to believe in himself; if he cannot do that, sooner or later he is certain to fail as a writer—and this may hold true equally well of the professional as of the novice.

The fact is, there is not and never has been and never will be a writer who has not from time to time doubted himself, or fallen into black moods at his slow progress, or come to believe that he is a failure. Beginners should understand that the creative urge in expression imposes great mental and physical strain on a writer, and that he is bound to have periods in which he is aware of a lack of energy, usually accompanied by mental depression. The obvious and only cure is a rest from creative activity until the writer is revitalized, of course. That the writer should react with diminution of ego at such times is as psychologically sound and natural as that a headache may result from eyestrain.

But the more serious doubts which assail every writer apart from these black periods need to be more carefully resolved. The beginner, often excited by advertisements of author's agents about the success of their clients, or by news accounts of fabulous sums made by writers—never recognizing that these are very often the exception, not the rule—usually begins full of enthusiasm, buoyed up by hope, and certain that he, too, will soon enter the magic portals of success, creatively and financially, only to find that the way is long and hard, and there is no easy way to the goal, which seems to retreat ever farther and farther away. I have often

been asked at lectures and other public appearances why I
began to write and why I write. An author writes either for
money or because he must, and I write, in common with
many other authors, for both reasons.

As to beginning—I began because I was filled with disgust
at the little filler stories that appeared after the "Old and
Young King Brady" stories in the old *Secret Service Magazine*. I felt that I could write tripe as good as the tripe being
published there; I could and did write tripe as good. And I
soon learned that to write it was quite different from selling
it. I began at thirteen, and I sold at fifteen. The selling of
my first story involved a direct challenge to the ego. I had
written forty stories before I sold one, and that I should then
have sold one was purely an accident of determination. I had
fixed upon the figure forty, resolving that when I had written
forty stories without selling one, I would re-examine my determination to become a writer, because I had read somewhere that Charles Dickens had taken his first book to forty
publishers before it was accepted. By that accident of reading, I fixed upon forty, and when I had written forty, most
of them weird stories which had been duly rejected by Farnsworth Wright of *Weird Tales*, I looked them all over, one
after the other, and endured my own private soul-struggle.
On one or two rejection slips Wright had penned a brief, en-
couraging note—"Try us again!" or, "Sorry. Try once
more."—and I read the stories thus rejected with especial
interest. They did not seem to me to merit re-submission, but
my eighteenth story did. I felt that it was honestly as good
as many of the things which Wright had been publishing,
and, if it was not up to acceptable status, it could be brought
to that level. So, firmly but politely, I resubmitted the story,

stating that I felt it could be made acceptable, and in response received a most agreeable letter from Wright suggesting certain changes, calling my attention to my error in the matter of the Cockney dialect, with the felicitous result that the story, revised, was ultimately sold.

Since that time I learned fairly accurately to judge when stories were being rejected because there were a fair number of stories on hand, and the editor could afford to be more selective; and in every such case, without exception, I simply waited several months, retyped the manuscript, and submitted the story in question again, and in every case it was duly accepted on some resubmission, ranging from the first resubmission to the ninth, an opening having appeared for it and the story being good enough for filler if not feature. Something like fifty stories have been sold in this fashion, though I do not recommend it as a steady practise, and cite it only as an example of a) ego, b) a certain ability to judge from the editorial point of view as well as from that of the writer.

Few editors, as a matter of fact, expect all their criticisms to be accepted without debate; that is not to say that they relish an author's taking issue, but they will respect him for soundness of judgment, which implies that a writer ought never to insist on a point out of a basis of prejudice alone. The editor is quite open to conviction; he cannot afford to entertain one half the biases and prejudices that an author may cling to with comparative impunity; he may have his taboos, but they are on the whole very minor ones, and imposed upon him from above or from outside. He will expect the author, if he takes issue with the editor, to offer sound reasons for so doing; he has no intention of posing as infallible, but he also knows that the author is even less infallible than he because writers all too often lack perspective and are bound to their works with all the devotion of an animal to its young. That may seem very baldly put, but it is no whit less true. The unconditioned ego does not permit of much breadth of perspective until hard and often painful experience has been brought to bear on the subject.

Not long ago I wrote a novel on a familiar theme—a boy from the right side of the tracks, a girl from the wrong side, versus small town gossips. The editor whose duty it was to send the manuscript to press for the imprint of his publishing house felt that the story was too slight; I had written it so fast, and at such white heat, out of indignation, that I had failed to really expose its implications or give it depth and adequate meaning; it was meant to be a serious novel and yet seemed to be rather a story of light romance. I mulled over this decision for some days, re-reading the novel, and decided that he was right. I then wrote him to that effect, sat down and wrote an historical novel to be published in lieu of that book, and then, two years later, undertook to revise the book, introducing characters from the village on the basis of their influence in opposition to malice and small-mindedness in their village, gave the story depth and considerably more meaning, and reconstructed it on a different pattern— from orthodox chapters to chapters embodying the use of sub-heads covering subjective or objective treatments of one character after another, and carrying the story forward in this fashion. I did not need to alter much of what had been written, but simply interlarded the newly written material, which amounted to about seventy-five thousand words as against approximately one hundred twenty-five thousand of the original. Much to my surprise, the editor objected that the new material interfered with the progress of the story, which would be better, he felt, if confined to the simple tale of the boy and the girl. His first decision had been very right about the story, but this subsequent decision was in my opinion dead wrong, and I remained adamant about making any further changes, writing several long letters in defense of the story and in criticism of his reaction, to such good effect that the story ultimately went through to the printers with no further changes save such as I wished to make and those the editor suggested to be made in the galleys, involving rather polishing than changes. (cf. *The Shield of the Valiant*)

The editor may well have been in error the first time, and so might I; he may have been right the second time, and I might have been wrong. But, in fact, I felt so strongly about the novel in question that, had it been ultimately rejected, it would have meant the end of a very pleasant author-publisher relationship of almost a decade's duration. Such a case is rare, of course; the book in question was, in the line of publication, approximately my thirty-eighth, and I was no longer in the beginner class fighting for my brain-child. Authors have been known to change publishers simply because a few words of text were changed by an editor, or for other reasons equally slight; this implies not only a colossal ego on the part of the author, but very often a basic instability. The wise author will recognize that perfection is a goal he will probably never reach, though he will naturally make every effort to do so.

In taking issue with editors, the writer should remember that the editor is right in most cases; but in no case involving artistic integrity should the author make concessions which cannot later be unmade. And a writer should never debate picayune issues; a writer who is concerned with small things ultimately loses sight of the broader concepts and motivations which should be his, and his basic ideals go by the board, while he dissipates his energy over trifles.

On Autobiography as Fiction

It is probably not advisable to debate at any length the assertion that every writer puts a certain amount of himself into his work. The author of even a soap opera is as likely to identify himself with his hero as is his listener, though not often in an autobiographical sense, as does the writer of realistic or romantic fiction. This procedure is seemingly inevitable because of the very personal nature of creative work, but for many writers it poses certain difficult problems, stemming from the danger of a writer's putting too much of himself into his characters.

The process of writing has been described before as a kind of mental digestion, which is to say that the writer creates out of something he has observed, concluded, read, etc., after his primary observation has gone through a kind of mental digestion, in the course of which the fundamental stuff of his story has had its essence extracted and reprocessed, as it were, according to the experience and imagination of the writer, who gives it his own individual interpretation and meaning. Clearly, then, insofar as the author is limited in experience and imagination, his creation is likely to be similarly limited. With equal clarity, it must be obvious that the writer's creation is very likely to be colored by his aspirations, ideals, compulsions, prejudices, inhibitions, dream-concepts, and so on, ad infinitum.

That this can be shown to be true is so readily recognized that few writers care to debate the point. Indeed, it may be said that a great share of the personality, warmth, conviction, character, and meaning of any given author's works is traceable directly to the character of the writer. The procedure, therefore, is in the larger sense by no means one to trouble the writer, be he beginner or professional. Yet he must beware of certain aspects of it.

For instance, it does no harm whatsoever to endow one or more characters with the writer's ideals, provided only that such ideals have a universality of appeal; but it is quite another thing to give characters one's personal prejudices. Prejudices are far more controversial than ideals, and controversy is out of place in fiction, apart from such crusading novels as are frankly propaganda. The reader who takes offense at blatant prejudice in a novel or short story, is not only unlikely to finish the offending work, but is entirely likely to avoid anything further bearing the offending author's byline.

I do not have reference to the author whose patent purpose it is to stimulate his readers to consider a social problem. Regardless of the author's personal bias, racial and religious prejudices, social mores, labor-capital relations, economic problems, and the like are, insofar as they affect democracy and life in America, not only permissible but commendable subjects for novels and short stories, and many fine works in both lengths have been written about all these controversial subjects. Antipathy to racial prejudice, for instance, is not to be construed as personal prejudice, any more than a dislike of hatred, bigotry, hypocrisy, and so forth. The writer should not confuse moral and ethical issues with mere social conventions.

Only a few weeks ago I took up a mystery novel and within the first twenty pages came upon an unmistakable, thinly disguised sneer in the direction of the late President Roosevelt. Had it come from a minor character, who might very well ultimately have become the corpse in the whodunit, I might have been able to overlook it, quite regardless of my personal conviction of the historical greatness of Franklin Delano Roosevelt. But it was spoken by the author's sleuth, his leading character and the hero of the piece, and manifestly represented the author's personal prejudice. With the best will in the world, I found myself soured on the book, and eventually gave up trying to finish it with an unbiased perspective, which resulted in the book's not being given a review, on the principle that it would be better to ignore it than to permit my review to be colored by the reaction the author had unwittingly aroused.

In short, then, a writer's personal convictions, if they are at variance with a great body of responsible opinion, ought not to make their appearance in his fiction. I do not intend to suggest that a writer ought to compromise with the truth; there is no possible compromise with truth whatsoever. Nor do I suggest that there is any need for compromise with the writer's personal integrity. I want to point out only that if he has an axe to grind, his work of fiction is by and large not the place to grind it; let him write an essay and set forth his views, and not practise deception by publishing a diatribe disguised as fiction.

There is still another aspect of putting one's self into fiction which is to be considered. That is the tendency to be so wrapped up in one's self as to create all leading characters in the same image—the author's. Any good writer may get away with this for a time, but not for long. Thomas Wolfe, for instance, lived so intensely within himself that he very seldom created a major character who was not Thomas Wolfe in different guise and with a different name, whether Eugene Gant or George Webber. His realization of this was given utterance not long before his death, when he announced that he intended to write a long novel which would be more "objective". There is in his work very little ground to believe that he could have done so; he had intended to do so with the George Webber story, but George turned out to be Eugene under another name, and Eugene was Tom. There was every reason to believe that the leading character in his new, "objective" work would also have been Tom under still another name. Wolfe, however, stands out as a superb writer, quite apart from his preoccupation with self; his was a vital, dynamic, brooding, dramatic, moody personality, colorful and deeply alive to every sensuous aspect of life, and every facet of his character and being is blown up to full-length and multi-dimensional size in his work, particularly his novels, of which his first, the frankly autobiographical novel, *Look Homeward, Angel,* remains his finest.

There is almost certain to be an autobiographical novel among the titles of every writer in the fields of realistic or romantic fiction. If there is not, autobiography is sure to form a part of many of his works. It is only natural that this should be so, for the author in these fields writes primarily out of his experience, and he is the most important and the central figure in any experience in which he takes part, whether actively or passively, and his interpretation is bound to be colored by all manner of intensely personal things—his latent fears as well as his aspirations, his training, his sense of self-discipline, his social reactions, his moral outlook, his memories, his concept of all the abstract virtues, and so on. No two people ever see anything in quite the same way, a well-recognized factor which accounts in large part for the fact that people are always, invariably the most popular subjects of fiction—just as, in the mass of whodunit fiction, the innumerable variations among people enable authors very often to protract a thin plot to novel length, thereby disproving a pet superstition held by many credulous people to the effect that the evidence of eyewitnesses is more reliable than circumstantial evidence, which it is not.

The autobiographical novel, done once by any writer, is apt to be not only an intense and personal book, but a rather authentic picture of life in America, a microcosmic picture, to be sure, but no less genuine for all that. Done twice, however, it is likely to prove only too tiresome. Precisely the same thing holds true of the repetition of characters, all cut from the same pattern and faithful to the writer's image.

Bearing in mind, then, that the writer of realistic and/or romantic fiction puts a certain amount of himself into whatever he writes, the novice will readily recognize that he is face to face with another sound argument for him to live in as broad a sense as possible, if not personally, then vicariously, ever observing, ever checking what he reads against life as he knows it. The narrow, barren life—in the spiritual and mental sense, not in the physical—is not apt to come forth with a novel or short story which will attract any great deal of attention or very many readers. The writer's self is only as interesting as he himself wishes or permits it to be, and by that same standard what he writes will succeed or fail.

On Book Reviews and Their Effect

Many a budding author, who has been watching the journals for reviews of his first novel, may be desolated by what he finds. Very often the kindest thing a book reviewer will say of his book is that the author "shows promise." That is something that is very easily said, and it commits the reviewer to nothing, since it is in effect saying that the rest is up to the author. The writer may find his pet novel torn apart, chapter by chapter, and may end up, after reading the reviews, sorely tried, if not downright discouraged.

The novice will find it difficult to correctly assess reviews, to take the proper attitude about them, and to be instructed by them insofar as it is possible to be. Candidly—and writing now as a book reviewer of over a decade's activity —the great majority of book reviews can be discounted in toto. The beginner may not know how to discount them, but there are various clues which are always ready and at hand, if he takes the time and trouble to look for them. He ought to bear some of them in mind, and fortify himself before reading the notices his first novel brings. Let him, then, bear these clues in mind.

1) If his novel is shredded with particular bitterness and without plainly stated causes, the reviewer is probably a frustrated writer, a great many of whom—judging solely by those with whom I have had contact—are writing reviews.

2) If his book is judged by any trite or hackneyed standard without specific criticism, the reviewer is merely displaying his ignorance. For instance, any reviewer who reviews a
book by saying that "this author writes too much," and not
showing just how this particular book suffers because the
writer is prolific, is guilty of a kind of fraud, since he presumes to uphold that old canard that where there is quantity
there cannot possibly be quality, thereby summarily dump-
ing Scott, Thackeray, Dickens, Dumas, and a host of others
into the ash-can.

3) If the reviewer carps unduly about details, he is
picayune and guilty of failing to see the forest for the trees.

4) If he blithely dismisses the author's characters from
the life by saying that "people like this don't exist," he
means to say only that *he* has not known them, and that tells
the writer with equal plainness that the reviewer is very
probably a self-satisfied, self-centered little man who is quite
content to spend his life in conscience-less ignorance.

There are others, of course, but the alert writer should
have no difficulty in the long run in identifying and watching for them. He should not, however, lean over backward
to condemn the book reviewer. There are book reviewers
who are not only very conscientious, but also helpful, and
he would be doing himself a disfavor if he failed to read the
reviews carefully enough to catch the kernels of advice
which, in specific relation to his book, could help him to
eliminate trivial errors. Having pointed out that some book
reviewers are manifest hacks, it is only fair to point out also
that reviewers are only human, and, being human, are just as
likely to be irritated by carelessness on the part of the writer
as any reader of sensitivity and intelligence.

The conscientious reviewer has something to offer the novice, and the novice ought not to miss it. I have found some of the least-known reviewers the most helpful, and some of the most pretentious the most stupid, arrogant, and fraudulent. The conscientious reviewer always brings to a book a new, unbiased point-of-view, apart from the writer's own or his editor's; it is a point-of-view of some little experience in the field, and is not to be lightly regarded. If his criticism of a book is severe and seems harsh, it behooves the writer to study it carefully; if he can find no evidence of any kind of bias, and if that harsh opinion is sustained by only so much as one other, he would be wise to re-examine his work as soon as he feels sufficiently far removed from the heat of creation and the excitement of its appearance in print to do so.

Once the writer has learned to discount bad book reviewers, he has an obligation to himself and to his work to study the reviews and notices of his books without allowing himself to be irritated or angered by adverse opinion. He ought to get over sensitivity about reviews relatively early; reviews seldom make or break a book, except on rare occasions, and the conscientious reviewer has only one purpose—to present a fair opinion about a work, as he sees it, and by so doing he cannot but be helpful to the writer.

On Fairness to the Reader in Detective Fiction

There has always been a great deal of pother and todo about a writer's being fair to his reader in the whodunit form, short or long. Many reviewers of detective novels usually have the author between a Scylla and Charybdis about this matter for, if he is meticulously fair with his reader, the reviewer is apt to come out with, "You can guess the ending of this one in the first chapter," and thereafter imply that the author is a dummy who ought to get himself a job washing dishes somewhere in an East Side restaurant; and, if he is not, he will be loftily lacerated by the critics with the charge that he is concealing facts the reader has a right to know in order to be on a par with the detective on the case, and the frigid inference that, as an author, he is in the same class as a confidence man.

Some of the todo has been warranted, and some has not—as in many similar instances. The late Willard Huntington Wright took time out when writing the Philo Vance mysteries under the pseudonym of S. S. Van Dine to draw up a set of twenty rules for writing detective stories. Good rules, too; the reader who does not know them will find them reprinted in *Philo Vance Murder Cases* (Scribner, 1936), pages 74-82, and in *Writing Detective and Mystery Fiction*, edited by A. S. Burack (The Writer, 1945). The detective story, he writes, is more than an intellectual game, it is a sporting event—"And the author must play fair with the reader." His rules are eminently sound, and seem to be incapable of being improved upon. But, he says, "A detective novel should contain no literary dallying with side-issues . . ." —and, irony of ironies, Philo Vance was always dallying in a literary, or an Egyptological, or an Oriental, or an antiquarian sense from one book to another, to which I am sure no one objected, least of all myself. And, he maintains that "no wilful tricks" ought to be played on the reader, and then he comes a cropper by playing one of the worst in the field, when, in *The Scarab Murder Case*, the identity of the murderer is clearly established midway through the book, but Philo Vance lets him run on when the District Attorney is ready to arrest him, long enough for him to commit another crime, and, incidentally, to round out the normal length of a detective novel, an occasion on which a good many readers of S. S. Van Dine did object.

Many a critic and many an author who subscribe to the Van Dine rules betray a wonderfully erratic inconsistence in subscribing to the belief that Agatha Christie's *The Murder of Roger Ackroyd* is a classic of mystery fiction, without apparently realizing that it is the baldest of trickeries in essence. *The Murder of Roger Ackroyd* is told by the murderer himself. Now, this gambit is quite legitimate, but when it is used, the writer is in conscience bound to remain realistic and credible in such a first-person narrative. The plain fact is that Agatha Christie's narrator *thinks* in a way he would never think as the actual murderer, and he thinks in that way solely for the purpose of leading the reader up the garden path. This is basically no different from concealing clues from the reader when the detective has already seen them, and finds them useful in detecting the murderer. It is admittedly problematical whether *The Murder of Roger Ackroyd* could have been written throughout in such a way as to keep the reader in ignorance, but it would have been far better to accept the fact that readers might hit upon the identity of the murderer in advance of the detective than to engage in trickery to prevent such an end.

The fact is, of course, that if a detective story is well and honestly written, it is impossible to prevent a certain number of readers from figuring out what is coming. Readers of detective stories include men of the highest intelligence as well as men of the lowest; the detective story is one of the most popular forms of entertainment that can be written, and to expect that every reader is going to be deceived is simply to expect far too much. The detective story is a challenge to many readers, and they accept that challenge in a sporting sense, try to put themselves in the detective's place, and out-guess him. The reader thus has a right to see the clues as the detective sees them; he has no right to know how the detective is fitting them together, for he is expected to do that for himself, and, if he is astute, he usually manages that successfully, and it does not—unlike the case of many reviewers —diminish his respect for either novel or author.

Like many another writer of whodunits, I had tried consistently in my Judge Peck mysteries to be impartially fair to the reader. As mysteries go, assessing Sherlock Holmes as a Class A sleuth, and Hildegarde Withers and H. M. as Class B sleuths, Judge Peck is probably a stable Class C detective, but, even so, I felt all along that too many readers of my experience too persistently outguessed the old man, and I was admittedly at a loss to account for this, since I believed that I had been reasonably devious, while yet being fair with the reader. It was not until both Vincent Starrett and Ellery Queen ventured to pass judgment that I saw light. The solution was very simple—I was being not only very fair, but "too fair". In short, I was not only putting out the clues for the readers to see, but, in effect, erecting signposts plainly marked "Clue!"

This then, seemed to me the crux of the matter—to be fair, but not too fair. There is nothing in Van Dine's set of rules demanding that the writer be more than fair, and certainly no reader expects it. I suspect that my own pains in this respect were taken under the influence of all the todo about fairness to the reader which I had read from time to time in everything from the daily paper to *The Bookman*. A similar influence may thus lurk in wait for the unwary writer who is prepared to embark upon the writing of whodunits as a career. I should advise him to let his conscience be his guide, and, if he has any doubts about his fairness to the reader, he can let some of his average friends sample the manuscript. If they outguess his sleuth by any large percentage, he is probably being a little too fair.

But the writer will recognize that it is better to be too fair than to be not fair enough. There are times even the Baker Street Irregulars must admit that Conan Doyle was not quite fair with his readers, though Doyle is an exceptional case, since the sheer magic of Sherlock Holmes is quite enough to more than balance such small flaws and inconsistencies as are to be found in the Sacred Writings. The deductive detective story, particularly in the short length, taxes the author very greatly in order to assure the reader of scrupulous fairness, for, by its very limitations, the short story leaves little room for the adequate examination of clues of such a nature as to enable the detective to achieve his usually startling effect by making his astonishing deductions. The novelist in the field is not troubled on this score by considerations of length.

All that the writer is honestly required to do is to permit his clues to be seen; it is not his fault if the reader is not shrewd enough to see them, no matter how much the author may attempt to dim his vision by sinking any given clue deep in the middle of a conversation, for instance, or dropping it casually among a good many other seemingly more important features. That it has been put before the reader at all satisfies the rules; if the reader is alert enough, he will in good time be able to check back and discover the casual or missed clues in plenty of time to enable him to fit the puzzle together and come up with the correct solution if not in advance of, at least abreast of the detective. And that should satisfy both the writer and the reader, since the reader has presumably had both his entertainment and his sport, and the writer need not suffer under the carpings of reviewers and will, hopefully, always get his royalties.

The novice in the field will do well to read with care such a book as Howard Haycraft's *Murder for Pleasure: The Life and Times of the Detective Story* (Appleton-Century: 1941) on the one hand, and anthologies like *101 Years' Entertainment: The Great Detective Stories, 1841-1941*, edited by Ellery Queen (Little, Brown: 1941); on the other.

On the Idiosyncrasies of Fictional Sleuths

The writer who is determined to embark upon a career of writing deductive fiction in the whodunit field will sooner or later come face to face with the problem of making his detective a "character", which is to say, making him sufficiently different to stand him out even among his fellow sleuths. The creator of the hardboiled detective has no such problem; the hardboiled detective follows a consistent pattern—he likes to talk out of the side of his mouth, his personal bravery is incomparable, he likes to drink (and will drink anything any time), he always has a ready eye peeled for a fetching young woman (blonde, brunette, auburn, or what have you?), and so on.

The deductive detective is much more sober. He is very likely to have no bad habits at all, though he may take a Scotch-and-soda from time to time, and every time he looks at a young woman, make no mistake about it, he is looking for *the* woman in the classic Gallic tradition, which is to find the woman and the motivation and/or murderer. But, since all deductive detectives cannot be just like Sherlock Holmes, the novice is bound to be hard put to it to give his sleuth something distinctive enough to set him apart. He is certainly not going to be as good as Holmes, either; so he will need some idiosyncrasies to give him color and romance.

The most sensible guiding principle the novice ought to bear in mind is that such idiosyncrasies ought not to be too unusual. In his earlier days, Sherlock Holmes was addicted to drugs; but presently Conan Doyle found that Holmes was a personality without need for such an eccentric habit, which was, in any event, offensive to many readers and essentially a weakening rather than a strengthening habit; so Holmes' addiction to drugs was omitted from the later stories. R. Austin Freeman's Dr. John Thorndyke stresses the exact science of detection by way of the test-tube and microscope; G. K. Chesterton's Father Brown is the foremost sleuthing mystic; Helen Reilly's Inspector McKee presents the involved and intricate mechanism of detection available to a large metropolitan police force (New York's Centre Street). Dorothy Sayers' Lord Peter Wimsey sports a monocle and is a bona fide peer of the realm; Margery Allingham's Albert Campion is cut from the same cloth in part, and is surrounded by a motley crew who help him to detect; Stuart Palmer's Hildegarde Withers is practically the only genuinely convincing and successful spinster sleuth.

Apart from displaying his erudition at every opportunity, S. S. Van Dine's Philo Vance likewise sports a monocle, drops his participial endings, and smokes Regies; Rex Stout's Nero Wolfe—incidentally, the most successful combination

of deduction and fast-action trends in the mystery field—
grows orchids and drinks large amounts of beer, all of which
contributes to his vast bulk; and, like Nero Wolfe, Ellery
Queen is an egotist, though without an Archie Goodwin to
laugh at him. The Baroness Orczy's Old Man in the Corner
sits at a corner table and ties knots in strings while he works
out the details of the puzzles brought to him. Ernest Bra-
mah's Max Carrados is blind (as is also Baynard Kendrick's
Duncan Maclain); Melville Davisson Post's fine Uncle Abner is portrayed as a simple, almost childlike man, whose
knowledge of human beings points the way to the solution
of the crimes he is called upon to solve. H. C. Bailey's Reggie
Fortune and Joshua Clunk both have many trivial idiosyncrasies, among which Clunk's habit of singing hymns is most
delightful; Poe's C. Auguste Dupin is addicted to candle-
light; Ellery Queen's Inspector Richard Queen takes snuff;
Octavus Roy Cohen's Jim Hanvey likes his gold toothpick
and strong cigars.

And so on, almost ad infinitum. The deductive detective
is, in short, very likely to have his idiosyncrasies or eccentricities, whatever you may call them. And the novice is certain to feel that his detective ought to have something different and distinctive about him, too, whether it is a fondness
for roses like Sergeant Cuff's or an addiction to mathematics,
like Dr. Priestley's, whether he dresses in a frock coat and
carries an umbrella, rain or shine, like Judge Peck, or
whether he boasts about having a "criminal mind," like
Edgar Wallace's J. G. Reeder.

But the novice ought to bear in mind that his chosen idio-
syncrasy should not be too far-fetched. It may be a matter
of dress, of speech, of gait, etc., but it ought not to be offen-

sive. The taking of drugs might seem bizarre initially, but not so in the long run—it simply does not wear well. Philo Vance's unlettered affectation of dropping his participial endings became extremely annoying, as one took up one book after the other in the series. Nor is it wise to overdo it. If Nero Wolfe had continued to absorb beer at the rate he consumed it in *Fer de Lance*, for instance, he might very easily have floated away. The novice's detective may have hobbies, similar to Elizabeth Daly's Henry Gamadge, whose fondness for old books has more often than not led him to crime; but the hobby should in no case take the sleuth's time away from the given problem.

The novice should avoid above everything else any suggestion that the chosen idiosyncrasies are taking or can take the place of shrewd and capable deduction, which is, after all, the predominant characteristic of the armchair sleuth. The problem resolves itself then into initial creation of an able detective who knows his business very well, with subsequent embellishments in the form of such eccentricities as may seem novel to the author, and are yet not so obtrusive as to eclipse all else.

On Writing Discipline

The writer of fiction, no less than the writer of any other kind of creative work, must sooner or later learn to practise a rigid self-discipline, and no matter how many subterfuges he utilizes to deceive himself about it, he must abide by the rules. The rules differ for every individual, of course, and they may take many shapes and forms, but the essential aspect of writing discipline is that a writer must form writing habits.

I do not mean to say that at nine o'clock every morning he must sit down to the typewriter or to his manuscript, if he writes with a pen, and turn out from that hour until one, a certain number of words. He may be able to do that, and he may quite possibly do it very well. Certainly it is a legitimate writing habit, and if he can do it, well and good, and if he can do it without permitting anything to disturb him, so much the better, and if he can do it when he profoundly wishes not to write—well, then he is a writer, and there is nothing he can do about it.

But I do most certainly suggest that he ought never to let a day go by without at least writing something—if it is only a series of letters, or a few entries in his journal (if he keeps one), or the expansion of his notes for his next novel or short story; and he ought, moreover, to have a more or less stable concept of how much he ought to get done in a stated time—a week, a month, a quarter, a year—not a hard and fast amount of words, perhaps, since wordage is after all quite superficial, but a certain degree or amount of accomplishment. To be a writer, after all, one must write, and all of us have been pained time and again by the would-be writer who is always talking about his grandiose plans, about his great novel—very often the hoped-for "great American novel"—which never seems to get past the first chapter, if indeed, it gets past the first sentence. The writer's is a way of life, and usually a solitary one, and to go around talking about plans for books with anyone but your publisher is certain to diminish them in stature and to take some of the shine from them in the long run. All too often the author who has talked about his plot for weeks and months finds, when he sits down to the typewriter to put it on paper, that he has talked himself completely out of the mood for writing it. Writing discipline is not nearly so difficult to impose on yourself as it may be imagined. Anyone with will power will experience no hardship under such discipline, but one who has not a sense of inner discipline to begin with is apt to have a rough time of it—which is a very good reason for redoubling his efforts at the outset and not taking every available excuse to get out of working. We all do it, of course—even those of us who have writing discipline. Faced with a particularly onerous task to be done, we are far too prone to clean up every odd and end lingering over from the past six months before at last reluctantly facing the fact that there is nothing else to be done but the task we have been dodging with such verve and energetic business.

The thing to remember is that in order to get into the habit of writing, you must write. It is something that cannot be said too often. And in order to get into that habit, the novice must take himself in hand and he must force himself to sit down and write many times when he rebels at the thought of writing. What he writes may be of no worth whatsoever; that does not matter in the least. Even if it is of no value, it has a certain worth in that it can be filed away for future examination if only to serve as proof that something was written in those early days. A writer ought not to be in a hurry to destroy anything, for that matter; but, once it seems to him expeditious to destroy earlier work, he should not delay.

The development of the habit of writing a little every day is the most important aspect of writing discipline, and once it has been established, other aspects come more easily. It is not necessary to put aside certain hours for writing, but it may be advisable, since it is too easy to put off writing exercise from morning to afternoon and finally to evening when it really is a task far greater than it ought to be. I do not suggest that the creative artist will thrive under such a regimen, but he will certainly not be hurt very much; no, such a pattern of writing discipline is manifestly of more use to the professional writer, who means to earn his living with his pen or typewriter and is not going to be hampered or pushed, as the case may be, by his "art". The genuine creative artist is never conscious, in any case, of his work as "art"; he is usually far too much concerned with its shortcomings, so obvious to him, that he has little time to think of anything else.

Once the writing habit has been set, the novice ought to fix upon his direction, though presumably he has had a good idea of what he wants to write even before he starts. Then let him write it, or at least begin the attempt. A writer ought to keep working along a single direction until he feels he has done as well with the form as he can do; it is seldom good to dissipate energies in all directions at once. When I was very young I made the acquaintance of a brilliant man who could play the piano very well, compose pleasant music, write poetry in English, Greek, or Latin, paint, and write fiction, and I imagined for him a bright future; but in fact, he so diffused his energies that he ended up as a college instructor, all his latent talents still latent. This can happen so easily that it very often takes place before the talented victim is aware of it. For that reason, mastery of direction is wise; a secondary or even a tertiary direction can always be established in good time later on.

A writer must learn to say no in a resounding voice. Once

his reputation is established, he is likely to be besieged by many requests for material, and flattered thereby, but he ought always to select his work carefully, and to know when to say no before he has overestimated his talents or his time. He must also be ruthless about interruptions, even if his callers are likely to call him temperamental. His friends should know his writing hours, and any interlopers should find out. By and large, he cannot very well afford to develop erratic habits or hobbies which are costly in the amount of time they take away from his work, but, on the other hand, he should never find it difficult to escape from his work and take a vacation from it when he needs one. It is quite as bad to be handcuffed to the typewriter as it is to have to be tied down to get some work done.

Writing discipline includes also the development of patterns for writing. If you write best with an outline, do not fail to make one before beginning work; if your story tends to work itself out without an outline, then write it that way. Learn to revise, even though we all know that there is seldom any work more onerous than revision of a manuscript. It is assumed that, having read everything foregoing in this book, the writer's observation will already have been developed, and his sense for the right details likewise. It is taken for granted also that the writer will almost instinctively examine the plot and manner of development of any story he may happen to read. Writing discipline leaves ample room for experiment, and, once the writer has got a sense of discipline, he will be able to do many things he would not have believed possible.

A decade and a half ago, when Mark Schorer and I were collaborating on a series of short stories for *Weird Tales*,

Strange Tales, etc., we wrote a story a day, in this fashion: I plotted, Schorer wrote the first draft, I rewrote and polished. While Schorer wrote story number two, I was rewriting story number one, and so on. In retrospect, it seems to me now that we worked with the utmost nonchalance. We wrote a month's stories that way, at the rate of one per day, ranging in length from three thousand to eight thousand words, and we set forth with nothing more to guide us than a week's range of settings and plots, so that a week's program actually looked like this:

Monday: Canadian setting. Werewolf theme. (*The Woman at Loon Point*)

Tuesday: New Orleans country. Zombie gambit. (*The House in the Magnolias*)

Wednesday: Massachusetts. Dead-alive theme. (*Colonel Markesan*)

Thursday: Chicago site. Voodoo. (*Eyes of the Serpent*)

Friday: Tibet or Burma. Cthulhu Mythos. (*Lair of the Star-Spawn*)

Saturday: Wisconsin. Malignant ghost. (*The Return of Andrew Bentley*)

Nothing more than that served as a guide to our activities. Yet, by the following Sunday the stories were not only all written, but very possibly one or two of them had already been sold.*

Writing discipline will prove of inestimable value in many ways—not only in simply getting work done. It helps to

* A selection of these collaborations is in preparation for publication under the title of *Colonel Markesan and Less Pleasant People* by Arkham House (1947).

develop the sense of detail, the power of description, a feeling for words, and, more important in many cases, for titles. Titles very often prove difficult for the novice; he finds it very troublesome to hit upon the right phrase to convey the feeling he has for the novel and the feeling he believes the title ought to convey to the reader. Writing discipline may well help him to develop his title sense, as it may help to develop assurance and self-confidence, which are so vitally necessary to any creative work, for without them, the writer is doomed to failure at the start.

Quite apart from the daily stint of writing you may do, the habit of keeping a journal or a notebook is a good one to get into. Many times it pays dividends to jot down a fragment of description, an incident from life which readily becomes the plot of a short story in adaptation later on, or some chance dialogue. All such notes are of inestimable value; it may not seem so at the time, but sooner or later you recognize that you have in them a veritable gold-mine of a kind of information you cannot get except by going out and grubbing painstakingly for it without knowing just where to grub.

Your writing habits should be an essential part of your life—not something imposed upon it and fundamentally alien to it—and they should not ever become a stolidly obtrusive part of your day, for, once the writing period becomes consistently a major and shunned task, the disciplining has broken down, and you will eventually need to start over from scratch, or at least, you will need to make a radical change in your habit-pattern insofar as your writing is concerned. Writing discipline should not remain onerous, however much it may seem to be so in the beginning—there will be days, yes, when it will be the greatest drudgery, but there will also be many days in which you will be able to do two or three times your usual stint and still leave your typewriter as fresh as you were when you sat down. Toward that goal it is wise to strive.

On Vanity Publishing

The beginner at writing is very likely sooner or later to come face to face with a vanity publisher. He will be approached with a plan to proceed with publication of a book of his work on a basis involving payment, either whole or in part, but usually whole, by the author. This kind of publication, whether it is by a fly-by-night book publisher or by a magazine demanding that the contributor subscribe before his contribution can be accepted, is termed vanity publication because anyone who unwittingly bites on it is usually labeled as being vain in wanting to see his work published.

The victims of this kind of publishing are usually lady poets, though occasionally the writer of fiction falls also. It is practised chiefly in "anthologies" usually of the "greatest" poets of this or that kind "in the world", and any lady poet who has received one of the flattering sucker-bait letters sent out by publishers specializing in this sort of play on "creative" vanity, is usually overwhelmed by the honor—enough to send in her contribution together with all the way from two to twelve dollars for a copy or copies of the book containing the poem. At five hundred contributors at say five dollars each, and at a cost of printing one thousand copies of the book at most of say one thousand, two hundred dollars, the publisher obviously stands to make a neat profit without a penny spent in overhead or advertising of any kind, save for a few "review" copies which are very seldom reviewed, reviewers being able enough to recognize the usually cheaply printed book for what it is.

The contributors to these anthologies, and the authors of such vanity-published books are very often extremely trying on genuine writers, librarians, booksellers, and so on, largely because of their loud and frequent insistence on their "unrecognized" genius. A lady in a nearby city, for instance, insists on cluttering up the badly crowded shelves of the local library with thick, bulging volumes of the world's greatest contemporary poetry—if such it can be called—solely because of her own contributions therein, books which are of no worth whatsoever as anything but paper salvage.

The writer should therefore be wary of such traps, and should make it a rule to contribute to no market, magazine or book publisher, when he is required to pay any part whatsoever of the cost of publication.

But the writer is, in final analysis, a free agent. If he is fully aware of the stigma of vanity publishing, he is at perfect liberty to go ahead and make the investment. And, if by some chance, he takes over the venture and actually makes money on it, he has the satisfaction of knowing at least that he is on the way to becoming a businessman.

On Helps for the Writer

"Writers are born and not made."

That is pure stock, hackneyed stock, to be sure, and doubtlessly it is being said scores of times every day throughout the United States. It is, of course, quite contrary to fact; there is no basis whatsoever for it. Writers are being made every day; they are being made by a great many events, from personal frustrations to correspondence schools. It might be possible to assert that creative artists are born and not made, but even that would have to be qualified by adding that creative artists are not made by instruction, textbooks, and the like, for the psychiatrists have very definitely proved that personal frustrations have developed creative artists out of people whose direction previously was entirely alien to the creative life.

My primary concern here is with the would-be professional writer. There are thousands of willing people throughout the country who believe themselves writers because they have put together a little ditty for a Club anniversary or something of the sort; there are thousands more who are writers by their own say-so only, and no other evidence; and there are hundreds who write in a manner so eclectic that they are constantly in the position of Robert Browning, who answered a request to explain a certain stanza in a poem by saying that when it was written, only God and he knew what it meant, "and now only God knows." But the young man or young woman who sets out conscientiously to become a writer has to learn a great many things not only about the actual feat of writing, but about all manner of aspects of marketing, copyright, and so forth.

Now, it is a truism that it is very difficult to teach people how to write, however willing they are. They must have certain attributes which it is impossible to give them. Try instilling imagination into someone utterly devoid of it, for instance, or sensitivity and sympathy into someone completely alien to them. No, it will not do at all. But it must be accepted that most people who set their minds on becoming writers are truthfully endowed with most of the necessary attributes. And these people can, to a certain extent, be instructed.

Of the various ways in which they can be instructed, only the individual himself can determine whether he will benefit more from composition classes or from textbooks on the subject. I had four instructors in composition at the University of Wisconsin. From the first I got the necessary appreciation to send me to the second, who taught me how to avoid ruts in writing; the third helped to broaden the scope of my writing, and the fourth taught me detail selection. Each one of these facets of writing was and is valuable; yet I believe that I got considerably more instruction from simple observation and deliberate, sometimes forced writing itself. One other source of information proved of great value to me, and it should prove so to many another beginner.

I have reference to the scores of books written for the especial use of writers. Not all of them are good, of course, and quite a few of them are specialized. Of those I read—and most of them after I had already become a writer, after the publication of five or six books and many magazine pieces—I found one book of outstanding value. That book was Edward Weeks's *This Trade of Writing,* originally published in 1935. There are also several other similar texts to which the novice can turn with profit, and I list them here in no particular order.

The Writing of Fiction, by Edith Wharton
Narrative Technique, by Thomas H. Uzzell
The Story Writer, by Edith Ronald Mirrielees
The Writer's Handbook, edited by A. S. Burack

The Craft of Novel Writing, edited by A. S. Burack
Writing Non-Fiction, by Walter S. Campbell
Writing Detective and Mystery Fiction, edited by A. S. Burack
Mystery Fiction: Theory and Technique, by Marie F. Rodell
The Craft of Fiction, by Percy Lubbock

There are other texts besides these, of course, but I have found these particularly helpful. The writer is advised likewise to get hold of some simple text informing him about matters of copyright, the public domain, preparation of manuscripts, and the like; and it is assumed that every writer will have ready access to certain fundamental books he should have—a good dictionary, a comprehensive encyclopedia, Bartlett's *Quotations*, Roget's *Thesaurus*, etc. These are the essential tools of his craft, and how he uses them may go a long way to determining his success as a writer. It will take time to learn how to use them; they are exceedingly helpful if properly used, and only something to take up space if not called upon when necessary.

But the writer will recognize that all the books in the world and all the best classes in composition cannot make him a writer if he has not certain fundamental attributes he cannot get elsewhere—above them all, the sincere will to do, to accomplish, to achieve his goal.

INDEX